IAN McLAUCHLAN'S
SCOTTISH RUGBY SCRAPBOOK

IAN McLAUCHLAN'S
SCOTTISH RUGBY SCRAPBOOK

PICTORIAL
PRESENTATIONS

SOUVENIR PRESS

Frontis. Firework thrown on to Murrayfield is kicked
off by I. McLauchlan.

First published 1982 by Souvenir Press Ltd,
43 Great Russell Street, London WC1B 3PA
and simultaneously in Canada

ISBN 0 285 62542 X casebound
ISBN 0 285 62543 8 paperback

Filmset and printed in Great Britain
by BAS Printers Limited, Over Wallop,
Hampshire

CONTENTS

ACKNOWLEDGEMENTS

Ian McLauchlan would like to thank the following for permission to reproduce their photographs in this book:

The Scotsman, The Glasgow Herald, Evening Times, Scottish Daily Record, Sunday Mail, Evening Post, The Daily News, The Sport and General Press Agency, Colorsport, John Rubython, D. C. Thomson & Co. Ltd., Alex "Tug" Wilson.

FOREWORD

The 1970s threw up a host of great rugby players all over the world and seldom, if ever, has Britain produced so many brilliant players and dynamic personalities at the same time.

Casting an eye along the top shelf of this *crème de la crème* of footballing talent, one would expect to see such glittering stars from the hugely successful Welsh teams as Gerald Davies, Gareth Edwards, Barry John and Phil Bennett. A place would surely be reserved for England's David Duckham and Ireland's Mike Gibson. And also perched up there on high, probably finely balanced at one end to prop up all the others, would be the world's outstanding prop forward of the early seventies, Ian McLauchlan.

He dominated Scottish rugby for the best part of ten years and developed into one of the most successful and most inspirational captains ever. He toured with the British Lions to New Zealand in 1971, in a Test series that culminated in the historic victory over the All Blacks. He was a key member of the all-conquering British Lions tour to South Africa in 1974.

I was privileged to play three seasons with Ian for Scotland from 1968 to 1970 and appreciated that he was not only one of the toughest, most competitive and ruthless forwards in British rugby, but also one of the game's great characters. Born and raised on the West coast of Scotland, he is a typical product of industrial Glasgow. Perhaps not all Glaswegians are embryonic Billy Connollys but many are, and Ian certainly falls into that category. He is a self-made man in more senses than one and possesses an impish and infectious sense of humour.

This squat, powerful chunk of humanity seems to be hewn out of a block of granite, but, incredibly, he was once a seven-stone weakling. He was told he was too wee and weak to be a rugby player. A vigorous weight training, body building and fitness campaign ensued and the end product was 'The Mighty Mouse'. One renowned forward in New Zealand before an important match referred to him, not as 'Mighty Mouse', his world-wide nickname, but 'Mickey Mouse'. In the event that player lived to tell the tale—but only just, and only after a second medical opinion!

All his life he has been a rugby fanatic, and his happiest moments and greatest triumphs have been on the rugby field. But he has led a very full life along the way and can look back on a million marvellous memories. He has never distanced himself deliberately from controversy and he is well known for his outspoken and forthright views.

He has a rare story to tell and no one could tell it better. Sadly, the game now lacks colourful characters like Ian McLauchlan, and that is all the more reason why we should relish his scrapbook.

Ian Robertson
May 1982

THE BEGINNING

AFTER PLAYING rugby for some 20 years at senior level, one thinks back to where it all began and all the people one should thank for their help along the way. The list is a long one.

I went from Tarbolton, a small mining village in Ayrshire, to Ayr Academy in 1954 and that's where I first played rugby. At Tarbolton I played football and I was considered a very fair left-half. My father encouraged the football—he had been a good player for a junior team.

At Ayr Academy, rugby was the only winter game and I took to it immediately. This enthusiasm helped me immensely and I was also playing in a good team. It's not generally realised the depth of rugby talent there is in Ayrshire—at one stage the Scotland team had 7 Ayrshire men: Peter and Gordon Brown, Al McHarg, Dave Shedden, Gordon Strachan, Quintin Dunlop, and myself.

T. B. Watson and John Ashton were the physical education teachers at Ayr Academy and they taught me the basics and also put me at lock in the school team. J. Douglas Cairns, the Rector, and Bill Beckles, a French master, carried on the good work and they instilled in me the belief that the best rugby is the simple, effective brand. I've never forgotten that.

I had three years in the school First XV where I played flanker or No. 8, with a few games in my old position of lock. I managed to get into the Glasgow Schools XV in 1958 and 1959. Those were my first representative honours and they made sure that from then on rugby was to be the be all and end all of my sporting career.

I left Ayr Academy in 1960 and went to Jordanhill College in Glasgow to study physical education and I went along to a rugby practice. That was my first meeting with Bill Dickinson, the coach to the College and the man who was to have the greatest influence on my career. But this was no meeting of great minds, no instant chemical mix, no immediate recognition of untapped potential. I was just another player fresh from school, looking for a game, and probably playing out of position.

I only just made the College Second XV where I was taken under the wing of John Cross, a great bull of a man who told me: 'This is not schoolboy stuff

now, son. In this game you must be able to look after yourself, so train hard, play hard, and you'll make it.' I soon learned what he meant.

The game was much harder and of course the men much stronger, so I began weight-training. This not only improved my strength but increased my body weight and made me more confident in my ability.

Bill Dickinson then had a look at me and astounded me by saying: 'You are not fast enough to play back row so I'm giving you a game at prop.' My first game in my new position was against Aberdeen Grammar School FP Second XV and I scored three tries. My second game was against Langholm at Milntown in the first team and before the game Dickinson took me aside in the dressing room. 'Hold up the scrum on your side,' he said, 'so that the hooker can strike. Block in the line-out and if anyone comes near you in the loose, tackle him. If you happen to get the ball in your hands in the open run straight and knock them down or set it up for others.'

I followed his instructions to the letter and from that day was never out of the Jordanhill First XV nor away from the watchful eye of Dickinson who guided my rugby career at all levels.

In 1963, I was selected for the Glasgow XV to play Edinburgh in the inter-district championship. Not unexpectedly we lost—their side was bristling with internationalists, whereas we had none—but I was picked to play in my first international trial at Murrayfield. The teams met at the North British Hotel, Edinburgh, on the morning of the trial.

I was to play in the Blues team and we went into a room with our captain, Mike Campbell-Lamerton, to introduce ourselves. Mike looked at me and said: 'Full-back?' I shook my head. 'Centre?' Again, I shook my head. 'Scrum-half?' Another shake of the head and this was too much for him 'Where do you play?' I told him I was his loose-head prop and he groaned. 'Do you mean I've got to get down below you?' How the hell am I going to do that?' But he did.

Campbell-Lamerton was a gentleman who came in for unfair and heavy criticism when he was made captain of the Lions in New Zealand in 1966. It was considered that he'd have a hard time holding his place in the team, but he was picked as a leader which he naturally was. The Army made no mistake when they commissioned him in the Duke of Wellington's Regiment and he was an inspiring captain for London Scottish and for Scotland.

That trial was my first experience at that level and things couldn't have gone well because I was relegated to the reserves bench for the final trial. I was

Ayr Academy First XV, 1958–9. Ian McLauchlan seated, second from right.

Schools Inter-City match: Glasgow v Edinburgh, December 26, 1958. Ian McLauchlan back row, second from left.

Early days with Glasgow.

In action for Glasgow at Hughenden.

told by one selector: 'If you were two inches taller you would be a certainty for Scotland.' I returned to playing for Jordanhill and Glasgow and although I had other appearances in trials I did not hold out much hope of selection to the Scotland team. All sorts of criticisms were levelled at me—I was too small, I ran about too much so I couldn't be working in the scrum, I was scoring tries. But I kept my place in the Glasgow XV and played for the Glasgow-Edinburgh select against the Australians at Hughenden. We lost and I had given up hope of wearing a Scotland shirt.

By this time I was teaching at Barmulloch College, Glasgow, and was supplementing my salary by taking children skiing and on Duke of Edinburgh Award hill-walking expeditions. One week in March, 1969, I was at Glenshee with a group of children. We were isolated. There was no television and we didn't have time to listen to the radio.

I answered a phone call at our skiing lodge and it was John Blain, the head of my department at Barmulloch College. What he had to say had my head reeling. 'Stop skiing immediately,' he said, 'you play against England at Twickenham on Saturday week.' I was stunned, but I managed to keep my wits about me until I got home to Bishopbriggs where my wife, Eileen, had a letter from the Scottish Rugby Union confirming the good news. I returned the tear-off slip accepting the invitation to play and prepared myself for two new adventures—international rugby and flying.

My instructions were to meet Sandy Carmichael and a selector, Hamish Kemp, at Glasgow airport on the Thursday to fly to London. I had never flown before and that day was foul—wet and windy. But I was looking forward to my first flight and when we climbed aboard the Viscount I discovered for the first time what a bad flyer Sandy was. He was very nervous and the weather didn't help but we got to London safely with Sandy in one piece, if a little white about the gills.

Jordanhill College Rugby XV, 1966–7. Ian McLauchlan front row, fourth from right.

FIRST CAP

IN THE early days there were no squad sessions on Sundays before the internationals. The team was picked and we met on the Thursday before the game, trained on the Thursday and Friday, then played on the Saturday. My first cap was no exception and we met at Richmond with members of the London Scottish club as our opposition.

In the scrummaging session on the Thursday I was against Robin Challis who was a very tough customer. He was bending and boring as if playing in an actual game. No half measures with Robin, but I was having none of it and I pointed out that it was a practice and that I wasn't interested in a scrap. Robin quickly changed his attitude and the session went well. I have always been grateful for his co-operation.

The Friday session was really just for the benefit of the Press—pictures, team gossip, that kind of thing—but I always had the feeling that we did too much. International players shouldn't need a hard session on a Friday—they should be fit enough already—and we also had a compulsory visit to the House of Commons on the Thursday night.

On the Saturday we went to a hotel at Chertsey for lunch and it was there that I saw for the first time some of the strange eating habits of my mates. I had tea, toast and honey. Wilson Lauder had cornflakes. Some of the others had scampi but Roger Arneil was amazing. Mick Molloy, the Irish internationalist, had told him that fruit salad was best before a game. Roger ate a whole bowl of it which was meant, presumably for about 20 people, then had a whole jar of honey on top of that.

We arrived at our dressing room at Twickenham at 2 pm and the next 60 minutes were the longest hour of my life. The first thing I did was get my strip on in case somebody came in and said, it's all a mistake, you're not playing after all. I checked my kit, and double checked, and triple checked. I did my warm-up. The suspense was almost unbearable. Jim Telfer, the captain, started his team talk and the nervousness got worse. My nerves were at screaming point. But when we ran out it all disappeared. It was a glorious release, like walking from a dark tunnel into brilliant sunshine. You could feel the nervousness and butterflies instantly evaporate.

I don't remember much about the game itself except that after 20 minutes I felt puffed out, but when I looked around me every forward was looking—and

Three Glasgow 'Caps' 1969: Dick Allan – myself – Sandy Carmichael.

(opposite) First caps train together: Billy Steele and I, 1969.

England v Scotland, 1969—my first cap. I am second from right, back row.

In action v England in my first Scotland game.

'Easy, boys, I'm valuable!' Bill Dickinson gets the heave from Sandy and me.

probably feeling—just as badly as I was. That gave me a bit of a lift. It was the speed of the game which had caught me unawares. Everything was happening about ten times faster than I had experienced previously. England won by 8 points to 3 but we had played well and had not taken our chances. England did and cashed in quickly on our mistakes. I felt reasonably happy.

The after-match function at the Hilton was a marvellous affair. I sat beside Keith Fairbrother, my immediate opponent, and as with most rugby players we got on well. The only sorrow was that it was the last international of the season and I felt that I would have no chance of consolidating my position. I felt frustrated, but there was a tour of the Argentine coming up.

ARGENTINA

THE JOURNEY to Argentina in September, 1969, was unforgettable. We trained at the Athletic Ground, the home of London Scottish at Richmond, and the session went on so long that we almost missed the plane. But 21 players and two officials managed to scramble aboard to find that instead of sitting together we were scattered all through the plane. For 18 hours we suffered as the Boeing 707 droned on to Madrid, Rio de Janeiro, and finally Buenos Aires. Sleep was impossible because of the constant jostling of other passengers.

We arrived in Buenos Aires limp, exhausted, and feeling sorry for ourselves. We had plenty of time to contemplate just how washed-out we were feeling because we had to hang around the airport until the official welcoming party—and the inevitable pipe band—arrived. But our troubles weren't over once we had been officially welcomed to Argentinian soil.

We reached the City Hotel in the centre of Buenos Aires in time for lunch, only to be told not to eat too much because a training session had been arranged for that afternoon. It seemed incredibly stupid but not for the first time I realised that things are not always what they seem. The training worked the tiredness, the irritability, the lethargy out of our systems and everybody was in a much better frame of mind that evening.

Argentina was new ground for the Scottish Rugby Union but the SRU had learned a great deal from the Welsh who had visited the country the previous season. The Welsh had arranged to stay at a plush country club 40 minutes by train from the centre of Buenos Aires. Everything was laid on for them, but after a couple of days the players were at their wits' end.

They had everything—golf, snooker, swimming, table tennis—but they were living together in each other's pockets. They couldn't go out and meet other people. They had no shops to visit, no cinemas, no theatres, no crowds. They were feeling claustrophobic. The SRU got the message and arranged to stay in a hotel in the centre of the city. The players appreciated it—there was plenty to see, plenty to do in the capital, plenty of distractions.

Training under our captain, Jim Telfer, was hard and often happened twice per day. We moved around different clubs and there were always plenty of spectators to encourage us. The only insufferable parts were the endless receptions and cocktail parties, sometimes two per night. These were murder with all the standing around, giving the same pat answers to the same boring questions. The Lions had the socialising part of a tour much better organised with the players going into receptions four at a time and moving round the room constantly meeting as many people as possible.

We had one marvellous little diversion. Ian Robertson, who was a horseracing fanatic, told us that he'd met this man who would mark his card at a meeting the next day. We all contributed some money and Robertson went off to make our fortunes. Lex Govan, one of the two officials, gave him £5. When Robertson came back from the racing he started handing out handsome profits to everybody but when he came to Lex Govan he said very innocently: 'I backed five winners out of six. Your £5 went on the only loser. Tough luck.'

We learned quickly that the Argentinians were a very physical group of people who respected you only if you gave as good as, if not better than, you got. The phrase 'retaliate first' must have originated here and this proved to be the only answer. Between the hard, aggressive play of the opposition and the hard, unyielding playing surfaces, we were being hard hit by injuries and at one point more than half the squad were being treated by a physiotherapist.

We were broken in gently in the games, playing a 'C Selection' and a Country Districts XV. We beat them easily but that was no preparation for what faced us when we came to play the national side, the Pumas. They came prancing on to the field accompanied by an army of photographers and admirers. They posed and postured like show horses for endless pictures. Once the game started, there was no posing. We didn't know what hit us. They came at us like furies. We managed to handle it among the forwards but behind the scrum we were wiped out by early tackles, late tackles, high tackles, and worst of all straight-arm tackles. Most of it went unpunished by the referee, who was an Argentine.

One of the worst incidents I've ever seen on a rugby field happened in that first Test in Buenos Aires. Iain Murchie of the West of Scotland was running flat out and that meant he was really moving. He swayed to go between the two centres, Benzi and Travaglini, both of whom straight-armed him. Their fists caught

Scottish touring team to Argentina, September, 1969.
Ian McLauchlan back row, first right.

his shoulders and Murchie was moving so fast that he went up in the air, cartwheeled, and landed on his knees. I suppose he was a lucky boy because the damage was confined to a broken collar bone, but it effectively finished him as a player. He never played again on the tour and never played again in a Scotland shirt.

The referee saw nothing wrong and we were incensed. He also saw nothing wrong with Colin Blaikie, the fullback, being tackled without the ball by one centre while the other scored a try. We lost by 20–3 and we sat in the dressing room after the game and contemplated the devastation. Colin Blaikie was a mess with scrapes and grass burns all over his body. Mike Smith, who was a medical student at Cambridge, stitched Frank Laidlaw's left eye and Sandy Carmichael's head. There were bodies all over the place but worst of all was Murchie. He was in a sorry state, in great pain and semi-concussed. He didn't know where he was. We were very angry and

determined that it wouldn't happen again.

We went on to Rosario and into the jaws of a strike where the strikers reinforced their action by running round the city shooting and burning buildings and buses. It was like the Wild West. The game was delayed by a day and that night we did something which when I look back I realise was extremely stupid. There was a curfew of 7 pm on the city and we had been invited to a reception. We decided to go and the sight of 23 people slinking along the sides of walls and through shadows while gunfire raged still gives me shivers. It was ridiculous, not to mention extremely dangerous.

We went into the game at Rosario on a war footing and in the first line-out the mayhem started. Someone had a go at Al McHarg and all the Scots went for the puncher. Blows started coming in from all angles. We gave more than we got this time and it settled the dust. We had no further trouble and won the game easily. The spirit had returned to our camp.

The Pumas B selection brought another close victory for us and we then went to Mar del Plata for a break from the capital and to prepare for the Second Test. The cocktail parties and the social whirl continued but we got through them because our minds were on one thing—revenge on the Pumas.

Again they came out like prima donnas. Again the photographs, the autographs, the salutes to the crowd, all the razzamatazz you associate with American football and its prancing cheer leaders. When they had finished playing to the gallery they turned and saluted us but we received it very cynically —that gesture was not going to deter us from our purpose. Before the game, Jim Telfer's team talk had left us in no doubt what was expected of us. We were far more afraid of Telfer than we were of any Puma. I'm glad he was on our side. He was the best man at 'psyching' a team to a pitch that I've ever heard.

This time we took the battle to them. Not quite a case of 'retaliate first' but a determination that we were not going to give them the advantage. Each side scored a penalty and with the score at 3–3, we got a line-out on their 10–yard line. The ball was thrown long and tapped down to me. I got it to Sandy Carmichael and on it went to Telfer, Arneil, and back to Carmichael, who had looped round. Sandy went over in the corner and we were 6–3 ahead, and that's the way it stayed.

We knew what to expect then and many of our players were in the tunnel almost before the referee had finished blowing his final whistle. A hail of coins, orange peel, apple cores, stones, screwed-up paper, almost any missile, descended on the field. The Argentine spectators don't appreciate any team beating their heroes and they know how to show their displeasure.

At the post-match function, Jim Telfer told the Argentines that if they didn't clean-up their game, nobody would play them and their development in the game would be retarded. The official interpreter, however, didn't translate his remarks in full, especially what Telfer had to say about dirty play.

Argentina came to Scotland in 1973 and I saw them play a Glasgow-Edinburgh select at Hughenden. I couldn't play because of injury but I watched two incidents which left me cold. Gordon Strachan, the select No 8, was lying on the ground with his head sticking out of a ruck when he was raked by an Argentine boot. It almost cost him his eyesight. Then Ronnie Hannah on the left wing was raked on the back when the ball was long gone. He was opened almost to the bone.

In the Test Match at Murrayfield nothing quite as bad happened although there were quite a few punching incidents. The Pumas played very well, scoring two tries and a dropped goal to our three penalties and a dropped goal. We scraped home by 12–11 and they reacted as we had expected. Gordon Brown was laid out in the tunnel on the way to the dressing room. He told me: 'I extended the hand of friendship and he thumped me.' Gordon's father, Jock, who was physiotherapist to the team, chased the Argentines into their dressing room. 'It was the most cowardly thing I've seen,' Jock said.

Argentina is a great country to tour but it's a pity about the players' attitude to the game. They have world class players who could contribute so much. Hugo Porta is one of the greatest out-halfs I've seen in the game. Any country in the world would love to have him, and the others who impressed me were Etchegaray, Silva, Alonzo, Miguens and Carracedo.

They are good—they have beaten South Africa at Cape Town by 21–12 and Hugo Porta scored all their points; we beat them by only a point at Murrayfield, and Wales won by just two points in Cardiff—but sadly it now looks as if their development will be arrested. After the fighting over the Falklands it may be a long time before any of the International Board countries have anything to do with them.

THE EARLY DAYS

AFTER THE tour to Argentina, I felt that I had established myself on the international scene. I had played in all the games and it seemed natural that I would be first choice, but at home Norman Suddon of Hawick had other ideas. But when the team for the first international of the new season—against South Africa at Murrayfield on December 6, 1969—was announced, I was named.

The atmosphere before and during the game was unreal. The South Africans were under attack from the minute they arrived in the UK. Groups of demonstrators followed them around the country in buses, picketing their hotels, keeping them awake at nights with their chants, never giving them peace to train or play. They stayed at the North British Hotel in Edinburgh at the insistence of the police. Normally they would have gone into the country to get away from the pressure, but the police insisted that they could protect them better in the centre of the city. They had to be taken by bus to Murrayfield to train instead of walking out of a hotel on to a training ground.

For the game, the crowd was kept to the stand and the terracing opposite, again at the insistence of the police. Spectators were kept out of the terracing at each end of the ground. It was a strange atmosphere for an international but we adapted. The Springboks were further handicapped by the withdrawal of their captain and scrum-half, Dawie de Villiers, who later became South African Ambassador to Great Britain. The game was close but we got home by 6–3. Sid Smith, our fullback, made his debut and scored our points with a penalty and a try. The Springboks managed only a penalty.

What pleased us most about the game was that we held a great Springbok pack in the tight and in the loose even though they had a back row of Piet Greyling, Tommy Bedford and Jan Ellis. That, surely, was one of the greatest breakaway units of all time.

France came to Murrayfield and all our high hopes evaporated as they won by 11–9, but we prepared for Cardiff and my first encounter with the Welsh. It was a game I'll always remember. We travelled, as usual, on the Thursday and stayed at a rather run-down establishment at Penarth. It was very uncomfortable. The beds were narrow and I felt I was sleeping on a board. But it had a rugby tradition—the Barbarians always stayed there on their Easter tour—and that's where we went. I managed to get to a cinema on the Friday night and caught up with some sleep there.

The day of the match was wet and windy, the worst conditions of all. We played with the wind and built a nine-point lead, but Wales scored just before half-time and converted from the touchline. It was a killer punch. They dominated the second period and won by 18–9. It was a sad night because we realised that we could have done much better, but greater upset was to come when the team to face Ireland was announced— I was the only forward to be dropped.

I was not pleased. I thought it unfair. We had held Wales in the scrums but had let ourselves down in other places yet I was made the scapegoat. I was on the substitutes' bench for the match in Dublin and we were badly beaten by 16–11. It could have been worse—at one stage Ireland were 16–3 ahead and only two tries in the last 15 minutes from Wilson Lauder and Mike Smith put any sort of face on the score.

The heads rolled after that defeat. Jim Telfer, the captain, and Wilson Lauder were dropped for the Calcutta Cup game at Murrayfield but there was still no place for me. However, we beat England by 14–5 to win the Calcutta Cup for the first time since 1967. Alistair Biggar and Jock Turner scored tries and P. C. Brown kicked two penalties and converted Turner's try. John Spencer scored a try for England which Bob Hiller converted. The win set us up for our visit to Australia.

Scotland v South Africa, 1969.
The winning try for Scotland. John Frame breaks
through a tackle by Greyling (6) and heads for the
South African line with try scorer Ian Smith outside
him. Nomis (14) is covering across.

Ian Smith sprints past the desperate cover of Nomis
(14) and Bedford (8) on his way to scoring the
winning try. John Frame, who made the break, is 13.

AUSTRALIA, 1970

WE WERE due to leave London on May 15 for Australia but on May 3rd my father died. He had been ill for some time. Should I go on the tour? Wouldn't I be needed at home? I decided in the end that there was little point in staying behind and I decided to go.

It seemed from the start that the tour of Australia was fated. First, the Scottish Rugby Union decreed that those of us who had been in Argentina were not to get new blazers but were to use the ones issued for the previous trip. The situation was ludicrous. Some of the team had brand new gear. The others were wearing blazers very much the worse for wear.

We left London on May 15 but returned almost immediately after a bird got sucked into one of the plane's engines and made it useless. We sat around a hotel for 24 hours before we tried again. This time we made it but again, like the flight to the Argentine, we were washed out when we arrived in Melbourne and again, like the Argentine, we scarcely had time to draw breath. Two days after we arrived we had to face Victoria, this time under floodlights, a new experience for us.

It was a dreadful night with the rain pelting down and the ground under water. Sid Smith, our fullback, left the field after damaging a shoulder and Tom Elliot, our best ball-winning flanker, had a cheekbone broken in a clash with Gordon Brown. We won 34–0 but at a terrible cost to the party.

We travelled to Sydney to play New South Wales, who were the most powerful State in the country, and it was there that we had our first taste of the curious nightlife in Australia.

We were taken to a bar down by the harbour. It was a really sleezy place, but we had to buy a ticket to get in. Our host told us to keep our tickets in safe places. We had settled for a drink when the barman called for last orders and cleared the bar. There were many dark looks and explicit oaths from our party until the barman told us that a stripper was about to do her act. The girl was, in the Glasgow parlance, a 'scrubber', but worse was to follow. The barman announced that there was to be a draw with a prize and that prize was to be the stripper. We didn't wait to find out if one of the party had won her but made our excuses and left.

We played New South Wales on the Saturday—I wasn't involved—and were badly beaten in the forward play. We didn't match the physical play of our opponents in the scrums and in the line-outs our big men, Gordon Brown and Peter Stagg, were knocked about at will. In the loose we couldn't match the speed and ferocity of their back-row men Greg Davis, Hugh Rose, and Peter Sullivan. They harried the Scots into mistake after mistake and snapped up any loose ball going.

In the centre, Stephen Knight and Geoff Shaw thrived on John Hipwell's quick service and had the run of the park. The scoreline of 28–14 didn't flatter New South Wales who scored five tries to our two by John Frame and Mike Smith. We were not only beaten but badly bruised, and worse was to come that evening when our manager, Hector Monro, was recalled to fight a General Election. It seemed that everything was going wrong and we didn't have anybody forceful enough to pull the party together. The signs were ominous.

After seeing Hector Monro off on the Sunday morning we journeyed by bus to Bathurst. It was a spectacular journey through the mountains with scenery that made you wonder. We stopped for a few holes of golf and a barbecue. It was the ideal way of forgetting what had gone before and the problems we knew lay ahead. On reaching our destination we were told that we were each being hosted for an evening meal by a local family who duly came and collected us. I was in a house close to our hotel and had a very pleasant evening before returning and going home to bed early. But one of our troops had a fair way to travel and returned to the hotel at 2 am. He said he felt he'd been all the way to Alice Springs and back.

The New South Wales Country XV, whom we played on the Wednesday, was supposed to be one of the easiest fixtures, but somebody forgot to tell them that. We really struggled and were tied at 15 points all when Colin Telfer dropped a goal to get us home. It was a great relief to our captain, Frank Laidlaw, to make a winning speech that night.

We went on to Brisbane to meet the powerful Queensland side and to visit Surfer's Paradise and the fabulous Gold Coast—great for the tourist but nearly fatal for the rugby player. We swam in the sea, we swam in the hotel's pool, we sunbathed, we ate, we drank, we lazed . . . Just for good measure some of us even had saunas. Did we pay for our folly at Ballymore Park on the Saturday. The referee, Mr Burnett, didn't help our cause as his penalty total of 19–4 against us shows, but we didn't really help ourselves.

We won plenty of ball but allowed our half-backs, Dunc Paterson and Ian Robertson, to be put under pressure, and so poorly did Robertson play that Frank Laidlaw switched him to fullback and brought Colin Telfer up to out-half. We managed to draw level at 13–all but I was penalised late in the game for supposed line-out barging. They kicked the penalty and once again we had lost.

That night we really let our hair down and celebrated. What we had to celebrate I don't know. I think it was sheer frustration at knowing that we could have won, at our own stupidity for losing. Many of the locals joined in—I think they wondered about those crazy Scots who celebrate losing—and we found ourselves all in the hotel pool—they in their clothes, we in swimming gear. Nobody minded and it did wonders for our sagging morale.

We returned to Sydney for the last two games of the tour with our list of injuries rather long. Frank Laidlaw could hardly walk, Sandy Carmichael had rib trouble, and Tom Elliot and Sid Smith hadn't played since the first match of the tour. I was named as substitute against Sydney but I was on the field before half-time, replacing Derek Deans who had injured a cartilege. I hooked against Peter Johnson, the Australian Test player, and thought I did creditably well. Anyway, the joy in our camp was unconfined when we won 27–12, having scored three tries in the process. What bliss after the disappoint-

ments. What a boost for the forthcoming Test against Australia. But what we had all forgotten was the number of injuries in our camp. It was a case of the walking wounded.

P. C. Brown had had his head split and the wound became infected. His temperature was at fever pitch. Derek Deans and Tom Elliot were certainly out and Frank Laidlaw, Sandy Carmichael, Sid Smith, Jock Turner, Mike Smith and Peter Stagg were all being treated by a physiotherapist.

We trained on the Thursday and to everybody's surprise Sid Smith said that he was fit to play. George Burrell, who had replaced Hector Monro as manager, was sceptical and decided to give him a fitness test. In the heat of the noonday sun, Sid was made to run up and down the field then round and round it. He wasn't too happy but he managed to convince George Burrell that he was fit.

The Test side was announced on Friday, June 5, 1970, and to my utter dismay and bitter disappointment I was again a substitute. I felt totally deflated, but I also felt just as sorry for Colin Telfer and Gordon Connell. They hadn't been picked either and they were clearly the men in form. Our places went to Norman Suddon, Ian Robertson and Dunc Paterson.

Immediately after the announcement, George Burrell asked the 15 selected to stay in the hotel while the rest of us went to a training field. If I could have arranged transport I would have left for home there and then, such was my desolation. I couldn't raise any enthusiasm for the training and took very little part in it. A boat trip round Sydney Harbour and the Bay area later couldn't even raise my spirits.

The next day as I sat at the side of the field, substitute for all eight forward positions, and watched some of the players actually limp on to the field, I decided that if I wasn't good enough for that team then I was finished—a sentiment echoed by Gordon Connell.

Scotland were beaten 23–3—until recently a record score for fixtures between the two countries—and the worst thing is that it could have been even more disastrous. On the plane home I spoke to Ian Robertson at great length about my feelings for the game and it was he who persuaded me to keep going, to get back into the side for the following season. It was good advice—next season I was four caps better off and in Australia and New Zealand with the 1971 Lions.

THE GOOD YEARS

THE ONE thing that Australia did was make Scotland realise that we needed a coach, or as the Scottish Rugby Union would have it, advisor to the captain. P. C. Brown was now captain and my old friend Bill Dickinson was appointed advisor. They co-operated famously to produce a highly competent team which proved very hard to beat at home. Having said that, we lost our first three games under Bill's guidance, two of them at home.

One of these was the never-to-be-forgotten match at Murrayfield against Wales which we lost by one point—18–19—when John Taylor converted Gerald Davies's try from the right-hand touchline. I distinctly remember feeling sick and absolutely drained when it happened. We had plotted and planned the downfall of Wales and it had worked like a charm until the last possible minute when they dumped us. Nevertheless that game heralded the start of a series

Iain Forsyth scores v Ireland 1973. Eric Greirson looks pleased.

(left) Scotland v Wales, 1973: Joint effort from P. C. Brown and Al McHarg gives Scotland possession.

(above) Here I come. Baa Baas v East Midlands.

which pitched Rugby Union to the top of the popularity stakes and made it superb spectacle. Our next home game was going to be too easy and so it was—but for Ireland who took us apart and won by 17–5. The Irish gave us lessons in all aspects of forward play and when we staged a revival they were gifted two tries from interceptions. It was salutary to be taught the basics at top level but it was a lesson which stood us in good stead.

The last game of that 1970–71 season was at Twickenham, the graveyard of so many Scottish hopes. But we sprang a surprise—or at least P. C. Brown did. He scored a try and kicked two conversions, one in the last minute, to take the score to 15–16 and our first win in London since 1938.

I remember the climax so well. Moving into the last minute of the game we ran a short penalty. I took the ball and charged into the England forwards. I was downed by Fran Cotton but felt the Scots pack drive over me. The ball popped back and was fed to Chris Rae who rocketed through the defence to score. England 15, Scotland 14. P. C. Brown to convert. It was nerve-racking but not, apparently, for him. I can see him now placing the ball, turning his back on it, wiping his nose with his shirt sleeve, turning back and ever so casually stroking that ball between the posts. Some other players might have kicked that conversion. Who could have done it with such superb nonchalance?

P. C. always maintained that often, as a young boy,

Peter Brown, Scotland, prepares to convert at Twickenham, 1971.

The kick.

Success – wins the Calcutta Cup, 1971.

he dreamed of scoring the winning goal at Wembley and that he knew there was no way that he could miss at Twickenham. He had great faith in his ability. That day his faith made an entire nation happy. One week later we made that same nation delirious when we did it again, beating England at Murrayfield in a match to celebrate the 100th International between the two countries.

England troubles started before the game when they arrived at Murrayfield to discover that their playing kit had been left at their hotel. A police car had to be sent very sharply to get it. Fifteen seconds into the game, John Frame touched down to record the fastest try in international rugby after a mix-up between Robin Cowman and John Spencer. Not only had we won the Calcutta Cup and the Centenary International within seven days, but five of the Scotland pack had been selected to tour with the Lions in New Zealand. P. C. Brown and Al McHarg

Scotland v England, Murrayfield.
Scotland's captain Peter Brown on his way to the English line to score Scotland's second try.

weren't available or it could have been seven, but Chris Rae and Alistair Biggar were included in the backs. It was the end of a very satisfying season for Scotland but it was only the beginning of what was in store for the future.

The Scots who went with the Lions acquitted themselves well, but more importantly they learned the pressures of playing at the highest level, and from that came confidence. Those who had been with the Lions formed the nucleus of the team for the 1972 season and from them and the continuing good work of Bill Dickinson came the best scrummaging pack and forward unit in the Home Championships.

We started off against France with a confident win by 20–9, then travelled to Cardiff to face many of our

Alistair Biggar in action.

Lions colleagues. It was a bitter and hard game. J. P. R. Williams, the Welsh fullback, thumped P. C. Brown while our captain was in touch. Brown was clearly concussed and as pack leader I told Jim Renwick to kick the penalty. This he did. Then J. P. R. had his jaw broken in a tackle on Billy Steele. It was an accident but we couldn't help feeling that justice had been done.

With 60 minutes gone we were ahead 12–10 but then P. C. did something which made me think he still wasn't fully aware of what was going on. he tried a quick throw to Roger Arneil who was taken by surprise. John Taylor wasn't. He scampered away and linked up with Gareth Edwards who scored. From then on everything went the way of Wales and they ran out easy winners by 35–12. It was a humiliation and we had played so well for so long. There was still a long way to go.

Scotland v New Zealand, 1972. A. P. McHarg passes
but Sid Going intercepts to score.

Hot stuff v New Zealand at Murrayfield.

Sorry, Al! Versus New Zealand at Murrayfield.

Action against the All Blacks at Murrayfield.

A reluctant fan with Dave Shedden, Sandy Carmichael and myself.

There might have been a long way to go but we had a long wait before the next international. Wales and ourselves were due to play in Dublin but the situation in the North was becoming worse. The IRA seemed to be on the rampage. At a confrontation between the British Army and the residents of the Bogside in Londonderry 13 people were killed. Anti-British feeling in Ireland was obviously high. The Welsh were due to go before us and were obviously unhappy about it. Finally it was resolved when a number of their players said that they didn't want to go. The Welsh Rugby Union called off.

The Irish then applied pressure—in the nicest possible way—on the SRU to get us to go. The SRU, to its great credit, decided that it couldn't possibly ask us to play in an atmosphere which it thought had been created in Dublin. The Irish Rugby Union assured the SRU that no harm would come to any Scottish player. Security would be such that not one hair of any player's head would be harmed.

We didn't go and I'm sorry about that. I think the players would have gone if it had been left to them, but I respect the decision of the SRU—it just couldn't take any chances.

So our season ended at Murrayfield when we thrashed England by 23–9. Nairn MacEwan and P. C. Brown scored tries, Colin Telfer dropped a goal, P.C. kicked three penalties, and Arthur Brown kicked a penalty after missing conversions of the tries. England's points came from three penalties by Alan Old. There was no Triple Crown and no championship that year because of the refusal of Wales and Scotland to go to Dublin.

In December, 1972, we came close to beating the All Blacks for the first time. The struggle up front was shattering but we were holding our own. We gave away an easy try late in the first half when Alex Wylie ran through our back-row defence. With only minutes to go and with the score 10–9 against us, Al McHarg, the incomparable McHarg, tried to open out for a last desperate fling at the All Blacks line. He tried to pass, but the ever alert Sid Going intercepted to run in for a try which put the score beyond our reach at 14–9. Going's try was actually scored in injury time and I thought the result flattered the New Zealanders.

Into the 1973 season, our first game, our first visit to Parc des Princes—which had taken over as the home of French rugby—and our first disappointment. We lost by 16–13 and the fact that most of the game was refereed by a Frenchman made no difference. The English referee, Mr. Pattinson, was injured and the French touch judge, M. Palmade, took over. He controlled the game, as he always did, in exemplary fashion.

February 3 became an important date in my rugby career. I was appointed captain of Scotland to face Wales at Murrayfield. We won by 10–9 but more important for rugby we scored two tries to their nil. Long, loud, and joyous was the celebrating that night. M. Palmade, incidentally, also refereed this game.

Ireland came to Murrayfield and we were expected to win comfortably. About half-an-hour into the game I side-footed the ball into touch, but Barry McGann fell over me. I played on but felt my left leg wobbly. I went off and it was diagnosed as a broken fibula. Hamish Bryce went on in my place and I went to the Royal Infirmary. There were two pieces of good news there—we had won 19–15 and a specialist said that I'd be fit to play at Twickenham three weeks later.

The specialist at the hospital strapped my leg with an elastic bandage and I went to our hotel for the after-match dinner. That, and a winning speech, I was determined not to miss. I stayed in bed for two days, rested for another ten, then started training for the big one—the match at Twickenham which would give us the Triple Crown. When I led Scotland out of that tunnel at Twickenham I was fully confident of my fitness, but just to make doubly sure I had a pain-killing injection that morning. A lot was said and

34

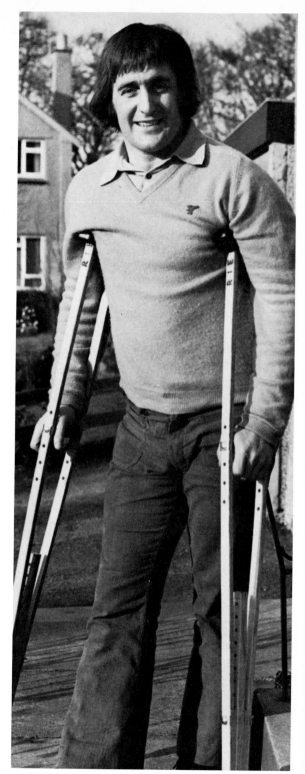

I'll be there, boys.

'I'll hold it, Dad,' says Scott.

Two 'old heads' together. Bill Dickinson and me at Edinburgh Airport.

written about my fitness that day. To the doubters I can point to the fact that I played the whole match and had a game every Saturday after that until the end of the season. I was fit to play. I have no doubts about that.

As for the game, we were 0–14 down at one stage but fought our way back to 13–14. We had the bit between our teeth, we had a momentum going, and we were looking for that Triple Crown, but a late try by Geoff Evans killed us. Evans had kicked the ball over the line and two of our backs each left it to the other to touch down. Evans didn't wait and dived between them for a try. England had won 20–14 and our hopes of a Triple Crown had gone.

Back at Murrayfield, we played a President's World XV to celebrate the SRU centenary and beat them 27–16, but there was no real satisfaction in it. We had the feeling that a season which had promised so much had fizzled out like a damp, pathetic squib. There was bad news for all of us that close season when P. C. Brown announced his retirement. Scotland had lost a very valuable forward.

Season 1974 and we continued our good work at Murrayfield. Argentina were beaten 12–11, England by 16–14, and France by 19–6. In Wales we were beaten 0–6 in very controversial circumstances. Gerald Davies scythed through the defence but was magnificently tackled by Nairn MacEwan. Gerald played the ball off the ground to Terry Cobner who scored. They were awarded a try instead of us getting a penalty. That was another frustration for us, especially as we hammered the Welsh after their alleged score.

Tonga came to Murrayfield in September and enjoyed themselves enormously even though we beat them 44–8. But they did manage to score two tries. At the dance at night we were told to keep the Tongans away from the drink, but they somehow managed to

(opposite) All clear after my broken leg.

38

Rugby at Twickenham. England v Scotland.
Chris Ralston (England) reaches for the ball during
line out.

Billy Steele scores against Tonga, 1974.

get hold of some and what happened after that was amazing. It's the first time I've heard my wife, Eileen, pleading with me to dance with her. The Tongans, with the alcohol gone to their heads, were dancing barefooted with any woman they could get a hold of. I don't think dancing was the correct word—each Tongan held his partner in a bear hug. It was all very friendly but some of the women were either terrified or had sore backs. Eileen eventually came to me and said: 'If you don't get up and dance with me I'm going home. I can't stand any more of this.' I acquiesced to keep the peace, although she probably suffered just as much from my dancing as she did from the Tongans'.

The 1975 season opened with Ireland at Murrayfield and we beat them 20–15. We travelled to Paris and lost 10–9 in a very bad tempered match

Drive v Pumas at Murrayfield.

where I had to have several stitches inserted in head wounds. The referee, Mr. Lewis (Wales), puzzled us with some of his interpretations and Andy Irvine had one of those days when nothing he kicked went over the bar.

Wales came to Murrayfield for a game which proved to be the last in which a spectator could enter by paying at the gate. Every game after that was admission by ticket only. Such was the enormous interest in the game that the official attendance was 104,000, but those who were there say that thousands more turned away when they saw the crowds swaying dangerously. It was the biggest crowd that ever watched an international anywhere in the world. For the players, the atmosphere was positively charged, electric. Dougie Morgan kicked three penalties and Ian McGeechan dropped a goal. Wales had to thank two penalties by Steve Fenwick for keeping them in touch until, in the last minute, Trevor Evans scored a try. In that unbelievable crowd I swear there was absolute silence as Alan Martin ran up to take the kick. I could not look. Were we again to be denied at the death? I turned away. The roar from the crowd told me that he had missed and we were home by 12–10.

To Twickenham and another tilt at the Triple Crown, but instead of glory just sawdust and ashes.

We did enough to win two games but couldn't score, and I will go to my grave convinced that Alan Morley did not touch down for that try that beat us. As we left Twickenham I said to Bill Dickinson: 'I think we'll come back tommorow and burn the place to the ground. It's jinxed.'

That was our last realistic challenge for the Triple Crown and it was the start of the disintegration of a very good Scottish team. We had a very good summer tour of New Zealand that year but we knew that the writing was on the wall.

Sandy Carmichael in action against England, 1976.

THE LIONS

I SAT IN a British Airways 707 and looked around. Was this really me? Was this really happening? For there with me on the plane were the likes of Barry John, Gareth Edwards, Willie John McBride, Mervyn Davies, David Duckham. This was 1971 and we were the Lions going into the dens of Australia and New Zealand.

We were confident. Our management team of Doug Smith and Carwyn James had done their homework. Before leaving London, Doug Smith was asked to predict the outcome and came up with a highly unlikely answer—Lions 2, New Zealand 1, and one match drawn. There was a lot of sniggering, not only in New Zealand but also in the UK.

The first Test was at Dunedin and on the Friday night Willie John called all the forwards together into his room and said: 'Most of you think that you've played in hard games. Wait until you see what happens tomorrow. They'll hit us with everything but the kitchen sink. They've got to win, but if we do our bit and win ball, we'll win.' He was wrong—they hit us with everything *and* the kitchen sink. Wave after wave of All Blacks came at a defensive wall of red shirts. I can't remember tackling so much in all my life.

My break—and one of the biggest moments in my rugby career—came when Alan Sutherland, their No 8, tried to kick for touch. I charged the ball down and, glory of glories, it sat there behind the line like a big, fat, golden egg waiting for me to touch it down. This was heaven. I did what was necessary and we had beaten the All Blacks. Not only that, I had scored the only try. Barry John kicked two penalties to add to my try, Fergie McCormick kicked a penalty for them, and we had won by 9–3.

Before the game, Doug Smith was questioned by the Press about my ability to cope with Jazz Muller, an enormous prop of 18½ stone. Doug coined the nickname 'Mighty Mouse' and it has stuck ever since. That day proved that technique can beat brawn. It was proved time and again throughout the series.

In the Second Test at Christchurch we played better but also made all the mistakes, and the All Blacks won by 22–12. Test 3 was played at Wellington and we ran out easy winners 13–3 because we played to our potential. The artistry of Gareth Edwards, Barry John, Mike Gibson, David Duckham and Gerald Davies, coupled with the coolness of John Dawes and J. P. R. Williams, was too much for the All Blacks. We were 2–1 up in the series. What had Doug said before we left the UK?

We knew that the Final Test at Auckland on August 14 would be do or die for the All Blacks. How could they live with the shame of losing to the Lions? In the final minutes they were ahead by 14–11 but then J. P. R. dropped a huge goal to level it at 14-all. Doug Smith's prediction had come true. In New Zealand there was disbelief, but it was true enough as we found out when we arrived at Heathrow. What a reception! It was unbelievable, absolutely rapturous. We were fêted throughout the country for weeks afterwards, but without the guiding genius of Carwyn James, who never seemed ruffled and who directed and developed our skills, it wouldn't have happened. He and Doug Smith, the archetypal abrasive Scot, were the perfect combination.

The tour was a great success both on and off the field and for this much credit must go to men like Chris Rae, Arthur Lewis, Bob Hiller, Jeff Evans, and Stack Stevens who although they didn't make the Test side contributed so much.

When the 1974 Lions party was picked I had a hassle about leave of absence because the trip was to South Africa. I was a physical education teacher at Broughton High School in Edinburgh and the education authority wanted me to act on principle— if they were going to allow me leave of absence to go I would go on full pay. They weren't interested in

Supporting David Duckham in New Zealand, 1971.

Jazz Muller and Colin Meads hold off the Lions. Sid Going passes.

letting me have leave without pay. I offered to go without pay but in the end I got leave and got paid.

Many of the experienced players who had been in New Zealand were on the plane to South Africa along with Alun Thomas, as manager, and Sid Millar, the coach. The know-how gained in New Zealand helped us a great deal. As in New Zealand, I played in all four Tests.

It was an exceptionally violent series of Tests with both sides often involved in brawls. Both sides wanted to win and no quarter was going to be given. It signified the commitment of both sides and I for one respected the Springboks for their pride. I'm sure the rest of the Lions did also.

The series was different from 1971 in that the forwards were the dominant part of the team. At training the scrummaging was extremely competitive and often had to be cut short because players were about to come to blows. This within our own party? It was unheard of.

This aggression carried on to the games and it was this same aggression, obviously, which started the fighting. Everything in South Africa was competitive. They wanted to beat us to prove something. We wanted to beat them to show that what we had done in New Zealand we could do in South Africa. But when I've said that the forwards were dominant, I don't mean to detract from the work of the backs. It's been said that we won the series in Tests where the game was played by our forwards, but on the tour J. J. Williams and Tom Grace, the wingers, scored 12 and 13 tries respectively, giving some indication of the width of our play.

Andy Irvine and Phil Bennett both scored more than 100 points—Andy with 156 and Phil with 101. Gordon Brown set a remarkable record by scoring

43

After the pig hunt in Gisborne, Fergie and I cook the prize.

eight tries. When did a lock forward ever do that in a series? Again, when reflecting, the men not in the Test team—people like Mike Burton, Tom Grace, Stewart McKinney, Andy Ripley, Tony Neary and Sandy Carmichael—contributed immeasurably to the successes on and off the field. Ken Kennedy, the Irish hooker, was immense. He couldn't get into the team because of Bobby Windsor but he worked like fury to get players healthy. I remember when Mike Burton got a bad knee injury, Ken practically nursed him back to health. Many of the players got a throat infection in Johannesburg, but Ken worked almost non-stop to get them fit to play against Transvaal.

I'll always remember the Sunday after the Third Test at Port Elizabeth. We were invited to Sardinia Beach for the day and our hosts kept us well supplied with food and drink while we relaxed on the miles of sand and beneath a hot sun and watched the inviting surf.

We could afford to relax—we had just won three Tests in a row, a feat no other British side had managed. But that was a desperately hard Sunday for me. Not one of the players went to bed on the Saturday night. We got to the beach and we were looking forward to a snooze, but Sandy Carmichael had promised: 'I won't let you sleep until Monday morning.' He kept his word. Whenever I looked as if I was going to nod off on that beach he would kick, pinch, or pummel me to make sure that I stayed awake. My ordeal ended at midnight.

The series in South Africa was won by three Tests to nil (the fourth Test was drawn) no other British side before or since has come near to it.

Sean Lynch with the team mascot, New Zealand, 1971.

Must have been a good one! New Zealand, 1971.

Charging down Alan Sutherland's kick.

Touch down for try in the first Test, New Zealand, 1971.

British Lions team, Australia and New Zealand tour, 1971. Author third from left, middle row.

In 1974–75, the Irish celebrated their centenary. It started in September with a tour of Ireland by the International Wolfhounds of which I was captain. We had a tight schedule, playing Ireland, Munster, Connaught, Ulster and Leinster in nine days, which was a bit much, but was one of the most enjoyable tours of my life.

I had fellow Lions Tony Neary, Bobby Windsor and Andy Ripley along with a multitude of French players, most of whom could speak very little English. But we got on famously. Jacques Fouroux, Alain Estève, Jean Iricabal, and Jean-Michel Aguirre all played a big part in the enjoyment. It was during this time that I realised just how seriously the French take their rugby. There was no chit-chat during training and they became angry if we were casual during the practices.

Being in Ireland there was plenty of hospitality and the Lions did enjoy that part more than the French, although by the end of the week there was a definite feeling that Alain Estève was moving towards our way of thinking.

At the end of the season, Ireland and Scotland played England and Wales to complete a momentous year in Ireland's rugby history. The game ended in a draw, 14–14, but it was a great spectacle and was a fitting tribute to a great country.

As with so many other aspects of life, being in the right place at the right time counts for so much. In the summer of 1975 I went back to South Africa to coach and play for Northlands Rugby Club. I took my wife, Eileen, and three sons, Andrew, Scott, and Ross, with me and we stayed in Durban for six weeks. J. P. R. Williams and J. J. Williams were also there that summer and Fran Cotton coached the local university side. Fran did not play but the rest of us did and managed to be picked for the Natal XV who played Eastern Transvaal in the Currie Cup and also Transvaal in a friendly at King's Park, Durban.

We won the Currie Cup match but lost narrowly in the friendly, although I did manage to score a try. These games more than any convinced me that rugby men throughout the world are much the same. I made friends on that trip and it gave my family the chance to see something of that wonderful country.

In 1976, I took my family to Canada where I played for and coached Toronto Scottish. The celebration of their 25th year was opened by a game against a President's XV. Douglas Morgan and

'Any quotes?' asks Norman Mair.

'You're under arrest, Dad,' says Andrew.

Wounded lion, Alan Old, hitches a lift while Tony Neary and Gareth Edwards follow on.

The Greatest (Lions 1974).

The Champions, 1974.

G. Brown, myself and Sandy—the mudmen of Cape Town. I was captain of the Lions.

myself and Tom Selfridge, the American, played for the President's XV. We were the only non-Canadians. Dougie had to go back home but the McLauchlans stayed for six weeks and really enjoyed it.

March 1978 saw Eileen and myself, Audrey and Andy Irvine, Sheila and Jim Renwick on our way to New Zealand yet again to take part in the Zingari-Richmond club centenary celebrations. At Dunedin, we joined Fijians and New Zealanders to play three games against select New Zealand sides.

The first, against Sassenachs, was played at Carisbrook, Dunedin, and this time I scored a try at the opposite end of the ground from where I scored

the only one for the Lions in the first Test in 1971. We moved to Auckland to play virtually an All Blacks team under the heading of Barbarians. It was played in the true traditions of that club because every ball was run. A feature of this game was that it was played on Eden Park on which England played New Zealand two weeks later—at cricket. The rugby authorities had to hire it for the day.

The last game of this tour was at Wellington against a provincial team led by Andy Leslie, the All Blacks captain. It was the only one we lost but it was not really played as a celebration game. Wellington went out to win and that spoiled things. However, the ladies had a great trip, the three men had a

British Lions training, '74. McBride (left), McLauchlan, Brown.

marvellous trip, and rugby benefited. Once again, men who play rugby mixed together to great effect, no matter their colour or creed.

The last game of rugby I ever played was again overseas. I played for Public School Wanderers against Zimbabwe in Salisbury and again there was a tremendous array of talent from all parts of the world. Fergus Slattery of Ireland captained the side. We arrived at Salisbury on the Saturday morning and had a light training session immediately on arrival. On the Sunday, we had a murderous one which really shook any travel weariness out of my system.

On Tuesday, June 10, 1980, at the police ground in the lovely city of Salisbury I donned rugby kit for the last time. We won. What better way is there to go?

I have played senior rugby for 20 years, twelve of which have been associated with the Scottish national squad. I have seen the world, playing the best team game there is, but most importantly, I have made friends all over the world and have enjoyed every minute of the training, the playing, and the camaraderie that is part of the make up of the game of rugby.

Still playing—but now in a celebrity cricket match for charity, 1982.

ritish Lions v Natal, 1974. Lions on the rampage.

At Hannes Marais' house in South Africa before the
3rd Test, 1974.

Derek Quinnell passes off the ground as Gordon
Brown and Colin Telfer close in. Mervyn Davies
watches anxiously.

Relaxing in South Africa.

Ready for battle. Trophies from South Africa.

British Lions touring side in South Africa, 1974. Ian
McLauchlan front row, third from left.

W. J. McBride.

Keeping fit the easy way.

Relaxing in the hotel with new cap Mike Hunter, Iain McGeechan and Douglas Morgan, March 1974.

Andy Ripley, '74

Determined Lions in 1974 v South Africa. Roger
Uttley, myself, Gareth Edwards and Mervyn Davies.

1974 – G. Brown and W–J.

Wolfhounds in action v Ulster at Coleraine.

After the 3rd Test Port Elizabeth, 1974 Sardinia Beach.

In Natal colours at King's Park, 1975.

Northlands Rugby Club, South Africa, 1975. Ian McLauchlan front row, second from right.

Zingari-Richmond Invitation match, New Zealand, 1978. Ian McLauchlan front row, first left.

Fergus Slattery.

NEW ZEALAND

IN THE summer of 1975 a Scotland squad left for New Zealand in a very confident mood. We had what we wanted, namely George Burrell as manager, Bill Dickinson as his assistant, and myself as captain.

Before we left, Dickinson did much work on the physical preparation for a tour which everybody knew would be a very hard one. The players were given schedules which many of us regarded with some dismay, but we met regularly to train together and help each other. We had a weekend at Murrayfield which brought everybody together for a very hard session of team training. We were all glad to get that out of the way. We found the most amazing thing about the preparations was that we were to be accompanied by just one Press reporter, John Dawson of the Tweeddale Press, and just one supporter. Vastly different from Lions tours when it seemed that thousands were to travel with us.

On our arrival in New Zealand we travelled to Nelson where we prepared for a week before our first game. The weather was fine, the training hard, the social life quiet, which suited us. It is during periods of hard training that the true character of a team shows and the New Zealand Press corps were quick to point out the fitness and dedication of the Scots. Dickinson, of course, charmed them greatly with his quiet and dry sense of humour. He soon won over the local boys, particularly when be began to talk about and demonstrate the scrummaging.

The New Zealand interest in the set scrum was a carry-over from 1971 when the Lions so destroyed the Kiwi forwards at the set piece that they could not compete elsewhere. Their interest in our scrummaging work was such that often all the crowds who watched us would be around the scrummaging machine we used. They ignored the backs, which we thought was silly when they could have watched the likes of Irvine, Renwick, Hay, etc., in operation.

When it came to selecting the team for the first game we on the selection committee had our differences. Neither Bill Dickinson nor myself had seen Graham Birkett, the Harlequins centre, or Colin Fisher, the Waterloo hooker, play, and we had no way of knowing how they'd play under pressure. We were committed to giving them a game in the early part of the tour yet we also had to play our strongest team in the first game to get the best possible start to our venture.

In the event, our spies had given us the correct information about Nelson Bays and we ran out easy winners 51–6 which comprised eight goals and a penalty to two penalties. We played well and everybody was happy as we moved on to play Otago, a happy hunting ground for me, or so I thought. This time, Otago set about us like men possessed. They threw themselves onto every ball and every ruck. This unnerved us which it shouldn't have done, but we still should have won. But to lose again to a blatant foul was too much to swallow. Billy Steele was covering a kick through when he was fouled—he didn't even have the ball in his hands—and Purvis was allowed to go through for a try which Laurie Mains converted.

We moved on to Lancaster Park which lives in the

Norman Pender and Sandy Carmichael inspect our plane in New Zealand.

Relaxing in New Zealand.

On safari in New Zealand, 1975: D. Morgan, D. Bell, Jim and Andy Irvine.

Early tour reception in New Zealand, 1975.

halls of rugby infamy and the New Zealand Press was interested in just one thing—would Sandy Carmichael play? In 1971 with the Lions, Sandy and Ray McLoughlin were the props and they were punched and beaten so badly by the Canterbury forwards that neither took any further part in the tour. It may not be known that it was not the Canterbury front row which did the damage—the punches were coming through from their second row.

Sandy did play this time and there were no repeats of the 1971 incidents. Again, we failed to take the game to the enemy, again we allowed ourselves to be dominated. We gave away two easy tries—one when we had taken a vital ball against the head—but what was really worrying was the fact that four tries were

scored against us while we hadn't scored one. This didn't augur well for the impending Test, so it was back to the drawing board.

We were also being badly hampered by that old bogey, injuries. David Bell and Colin Telfer were so badly hurt that neither took any further part in the playing side of the tour. They were delegated to bear the brunt of the socialising which David Bell said was much more physically demanding than playing.

As we moved to Napier for the match against Hawkes Bay we knew it was make or break time for the tour. Defeat would have meant disaster and loss of public interest. We were smarting from some of the Press comments but most of all we were hurt by Bill Dickinson's comments. He was disgusted by our performances against Otago and Canterbury and said so. But he knew what he was doing. There's

Welcome to Nelson, New Zealand, 1975.

supported every attack. Fisher was into everything. His front on, dead stop tackle on a huge prop called Dunstan was one of the features of the game in which we scored 30 points, including five tries, and conceded none. We were back on the road, none too soon, and we celebrated well.

At Napier, I realised one of the greatest differences between a Lions and a Scotland tour. In 1971, on the morning of the game, there was a huge parade of floats with about 50 lorries taking part. I told our party all about it and prepared them for the display. This time one float turned up with a very tired and careworn Nessie on the back. To make it worse this shabby creation had 'LOCK NESS MONSTER' written on her back. I wasn't allowed to forget that in a hurry.

Wellington provided us with the best game of the tour. It was a bright sunny day, ideal for the running rugby we wanted to play. The fact that we won by 36–25 shows that both sides gave the ball plenty of air. But there were a couple of unsavoury incidents, both involving Andy Irvine and Graeme Williams, the Wellington flanker. First, Williams late-tackled Andy and then he high-tackled him. This left Irvine dazed and his contribution thereafter was naturally muted. I felt that the referee, Mr. McMullen, should have sent Williams off the pitch because his actions were dangerous and marred an otherwise great game in which Dougie Morgan scored 24 points and we managed three tries.

Bay of Plenty was our last provincial game. We won by 16–10 and we were glad to get it out of the way. It appeared to us that they were trying to soften us up for the Test. The All Black flanker, Alaistair McNaughton, who in 1971 conceded a penalty for a late tackle on Barry John, looked as if he wanted to maim Ian McGeechan. But 'Geech' is an elusive character on a rugby field and was in trouble only once when McNaughton punched him on the back on his way to a line-out. We moved to Auckland for the Test, brimful of confidence.

On every tour when selections are made the players not picked are disappointed. It was no different in New Zealand. Injury had eliminated George Mackie, Mike Biggar, David Bell and Colin Telfer. The choice in certain areas was extremely limited. Andy Irvine or Bruce Hay at fullback? John Frame or Graham Birkett in the centre? Duncan Madsen or Colin Fisher to hook? It was decided after much heartsearching to play Bruce Hay at fullback, Andy Irvine on the wing, Birkett in the centre, and Fisher as hooker. Three new caps to face the All Blacks, but

nobody better than Dickinson at hitting where it hurts and yet lifting players to heights. We gave Graham Birkett and Colin Fisher their first games and they were inspired. Birkett tackled like fury and

Scrum v Australia.

Spot the ball v Australia.

An Australian is sandwiched between Gordon Brown and myself.

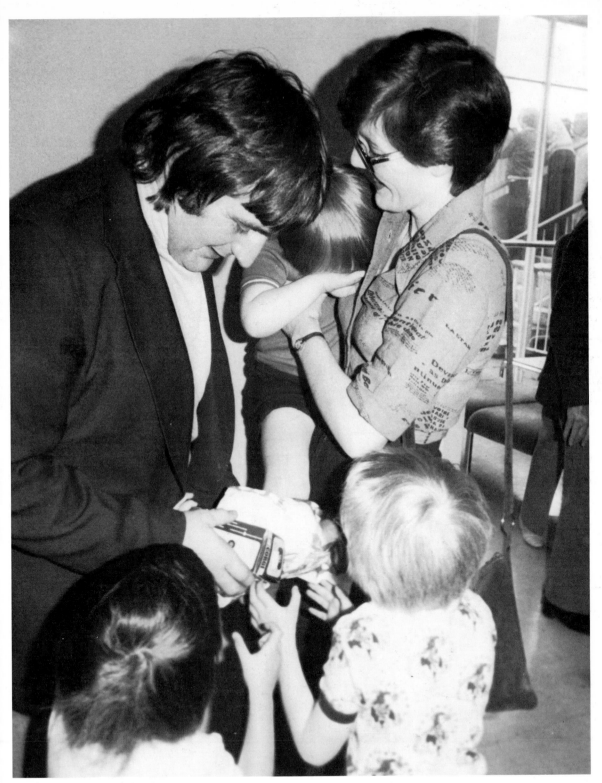

Return from New Zealand, 1975.

while it's difficult to leave out established players you must use the men in form.

The weather at Auckland was great, warm and dry. Just what we—and especially our backs—wanted. The All Blacks were also having injury problems, including their great centre, the classy Bruce Robertson. Their selectors decided to bring in Lin Jaffray and Bill Osborne. In the pack there was no Peter Whiting and this further boosted our confidence. We thought we would win and, more importantly, so did the New Zealand Press. What we didn't bargain for was the tropical storm which hit Auckland that Saturday morning, June 14th, 1975. It put Eden Park under eight inches of water and there were hurried conferences to decide if the game should go on. We would have been happy to delay it but the New Zealand authorities explained that people would already be on the move from hundreds of miles distant to see the game. It had to go on. It did go on and was rightly named the Water Polo Test.

We didn't adapt our game. How do you adapt to playing when water is lapping over your boots? How do you adapt to feeling that you're going to drown every time you fall? But our forward play was loose and the backs made many mistakes. Bruce Hay had his right arm broken early in the game. Andy Irvine switched to fullback and Billy Steele came on to the wing. The All Blacks pumped the ball up into the air and chased. They tackled and harried us into more and more mistakes and finally won by four goals to nil. It was a bitterly disappointing way to end such a happy trip. If it had been dry we would have won—or would we? We were convinced we would have done.

We made many friends. We were told that we were the best behaved tourists to have visited New Zealand and were tremendous ambassadors for Scotland. The manager, George Burrell, did a very good job aided amiably by Bill Dickinson who won a new host of admirers in that rugby-mad country. It was a great trip and of great value to Scottish rugby.

THE LEAN YEARS

AFTER THE great tour of New Zealand everybody was buzzing and ready for the big challenges of the new international season. We met the Australians at Murrayfield on December 6, 1975, and this was a landmark in the great career of Sandy Carmichael. He led the Scottish team on to Murrayfield that afternoon in honour of his 41st cap—a record for a Scotland forward.

We beat Australia but this time two of our scores were hotly disputed. Lewis Dick went over in the corner with a tackler hanging round his legs and fortunately for us the referee, Mr. Johnston of England, decided that the tackler was in touch and not the ball. The second try came from an interception. Some of the Australians thought that Ian McGeechan knocked-on when he took the ball. McGeechan didn't wait to hear the Australian protests—he sent Jim Renwick scampering away for a try which Dougie Morgan converted. Paul McLean kicked a penalty for the visitors, but we had had huge amounts of possession and the failure to turn it into points made us uneasy. We got our first international of that season under our belts, though, with a win by 10–3.

The start of the Home International championships proved that our unease was not misplaced. France came to Murrayfield and returned to Paris with a win by 13 points to 6. Again, we were all over our opponents as far as possession was concerned but again we couldn't score and again there was controversy. Andy Irvine lined up to kick at goal from about the half-way, but the ball kept blowing over. I held it for him and he kicked the penalty but to the crowd's dismay and our anger the referee, Mr. Pattinson of England, disallowed it by saying that I was lying in front of the ball when I was holding it and was therefore offside.

He admitted later that he was wrong and offered his apologies. I was very angry. If that kick had been allowed we felt sure that we would have gone on and won, and so maintained our record of ten home wins in a row. It was a very strange incident and I don't think the rules say anything about that kind of offside.

Three weeks later in Cardiff, there was more refereeing controversy which reduced the match to a farce. Dr. Cuny, a Frenchman, was in charge and early in the game he injured a leg. Mervyn Davies, the Welsh captain, and myself pleaded with him to go off but he refused. It was ridiculous. He was continuously 50 yards behind play. He'd whistle for a scrum—how he knew what was going on from 50 yards I'll never know—then arrive about a minute later to supervise the put-in. It was no joke because some of the forward exchanges were raw and at that time the touch judge had no power to indicate misconduct. The Dr. Cuny situation couldn't happen

Warm-up at Murrayfield before training.

Interception v France at Murrayfield.

Engaging the foe. Australia, 1976.

A very proud moment.

Presentation from the President of the Calcutta Club – Calcutta Cup.

now but the good doctor was obviously determined to make his one and only international appearance last a long time. We lost the game by 28–6. Wales would have beaten us anyway, but the way the game was handled was more of an irritant to us than losing.

But we did salvage something from the season—we beat England 22–12 at Murrayfield, then achieved something very rare when we won an away game, beating Ireland in Dublin 15–6.

The England game was particularly gratifying since it was a Royal occasion with the Queen and Prince Philip as spectators. I am an unashamed Royalist and I loved it. What makes me angry now is the whistling and the jeering when the National Anthem is played at Murrayfield. I suppose it's inevitable that the National Anthem will be dropped in favour of a Scottish Anthem one day, but until that

happens why don't the louts stop insulting the Queen?

Early on, the English pack were giving us a good hiding and they had moved into a lead of 9 points to 3 when Dave Shedden caught a high kick inside our 22 and started to run. He passed to Mike Biggar, and on the ball went to the hands of Sandy Carmichael, Alan Tomes, and finally Alan Lawson who scored near the posts. Andy Irvine converted and we were level, but that score did something more important—it took the heart out of England and Lawson and David Leslie scored again to give us another Calcutta Cup win.

Our away win against Ireland—our first since 1971—was described as 80 minutes of unrelieved boredom. Andy Irvine kicked four penalties and Ron Wilson dropped a goal for our 15 points. Barry McGann had two penalties for Ireland. The game

The old firm: myself and Sandy.

Gordon Strachan in determined mood v England, 1977.

was played in a steady downpour and Lansdowne Road became very heavy. Maybe it was neither pretty nor entertaining to watch but it was a very satisfying game for the players and the result justified our strategy of keeping it tight. If the players were happy the selectors were delighted. They saw it as the rescue job of the season.

The end of that season saw Sandy Carmichael, Al McHarg, and myself being referred to as veterans. I resented it. I was 34 but I felt as good as ever and as I was the oldest of the three why shouldn't the other two go on with me? But it didn't need a diviner to know that the search was on for replacements for an ageing Scotland pack. What we couldn't foresee was that Gordon Brown would never again play for Scotland. Age had nothing to do with it.

Gordon was playing for Glasgow against North and Midlands in an inter-district match at Murrayfield. He got into a fight with Alan Hardie, the North Midlands hooker, and both were sent off. What made it look even worse was that the match was televised and BBC showed over and over again Gordon chasing Hardie after a ruck and grappling with him. Gordon was suspended for four months which put him out of the coming international season, while Hardie had a 'holiday' of 18 months. Gordon didn't do Scotland's chances any good by his rush of blood to the head. He made one further tour with the Lions, to New Zealand in 1977, but his career with Scotland was over.

Japan came to Murrayfield in September and this allowed new men to be tried. We went into a Trial in December and after it I got that old slow-burning feeling that I'd experienced before. I was dropped, not just from the team but also from the squad. Once again I was the outcast. I felt, and still feel, that it was my abrasive captaincy that upset the selectors rather than my playing ability. The ability had been proved time and again on every major rugby ground in the world.

January, 1977, and Scotland travelled to Twickenham with a much recast team which was comprehensively beaten, especially forward. On their way to a record win by 26–6, England scored four tries and two penalties and converted two of the tries. But perhaps more significantly, Alistair Hignell, the England fullback, missed a further five penalties, an almost unheard of thing for him. That gives a better idea of how far ahead England were.

Immediately, the cries from the Press went up that either I should be recalled or that Sandy Carmichael should be switched to the loose-head and Norman Pender, the massive Hawick prop, be brought into the tight-head. The selectors did neither but instead dropped Carmichael and the flankers, Wilson Lauder and Alex Brewster, and Alan Tomes from the second-row. Bill Watson and Mike Biggar came in on the flanks and Ian Barnes replaced his clubmate Tomes. Pender replaced Sandy Carmichael who was named as substitute, but there was still no place for me, even in the squad.

This team, with eight changes, went out to face Ireland at Murrayfield with, I suspect, more hope than expectation. Norman Pender's international lasted 15 minutes until he broke some ribs and Sandy took his place. Scotland won by 21–18 so things looked a bit better and I was restored to the bench for the game in Paris. But as at Twickenham, the pack showed very little enthusiasm for the fight and were torn apart by the French. The win by the French by 23 points to 3 was the biggest win by them in the series to date.

After the game I ran into the changing room, washed as quickly as possible, and left to wait outside. I knew that many of the players were upset. They had played badly, had shown no fight, and had gone meek as lambs to the slaughter. This was no time to intrude on team grief. There was no escape from a post-mortem later, though, at the dinner. There was dispute and argument, not just about the French game but about the whole season. We eventually realised that nothing we had to say was going to make the slightest bit of difference, so we took a lot of drinks on board and went out on the spree in Paris. Some of

Wilson Lauder climbs high v England.

the grey faces next day—including mine—were pitiful to behold.

The last game of the season was against Wales at Murrayfield and the selectors were in a fix. They had already made so many changes. Where could they go next? For a start they broke with tradition and announced that the team would be named in the dressing room at Murrayfield at a squad session on the Sunday before the Welsh game. Gordon Brown had been recalled to the squad so it was assumed that he would play. There had been much space given in the Press to his training with Glasgow Rangers at Ibrox after his suspension and he had declared himself fit.

The squad of 36 players sat round the dressing room and in came the Big Five—Tom Pearson, Ian MacGregor, Robin Charters, Alex Harper, and George Thomson. It was agony for me. What must it have been like for the younger players?

There were sensations. Gordon Brown was ignored and I was recalled, so four of the famous front five—Carmichael, Madsen, myself and Al McHarg—were back in operation. And what a hammering we gave Wales up front even though we did lose by 18–9. We rucked them off the park and only the brilliance of their backs and some great cover tackling by Terry Cobner kept them in the game. But when the Lions for 1977 were announced, not one of the Scottish pack of that day was picked. Seven of the Welshmen, who we had badly mauled, were. A strange world indeed.

Scotland v Wales, 1977. Seven pictures recalling a great battle, Wales won 18–9.

THE FAR EAST

IN THE autumn of 1977 I was in a plane bound for the Far East for one of the most enjoyable tours I've ever been on. It was enjoyable because we were on our way to Bangkok, Hong Kong and Tokyo, exciting places and new ground for a Scottish rugby team. It was also a pleasure because it wasn't a pressure trip. We were expected to win easily and we could enjoy ourselves.

Japan had been to Murrayfield the year before and we had managed, with some difficulty, to beat them 34–9. Sandy Carmichael and myself were 'rested' that day. I took Eileen and the boys away for the weekend but I finished up in the lounge of our hotel at Blairgowrie watching the game on television.

There were two important factors among those who got aboard that plane for Bangkok. There were a lot of young players and they saw it as their big chance. For Nairn MacEwan, the coach, Tom Pearson, the manager, and George Thomson, the assistant manager, it was their first time in harness and they wanted it to be successful. There were also, of course, old 'lags' like myself who were expected to bring on the youngsters, but my pride wouldn't allow me to go on the tour and not want to play in all the games, and play well.

We had a large bonus in that party in the shape of Brigadier Frank Coutts, the president of the SRU. I can best describe him as a man who is really 'laid-back'—he never flusters, never worries. Give him a pipe, some peace, some company, and he is one of the most interesting men I've ever met. The Japanese thought he was unbelievable when he led us on to the field playing the pipes and wearing the kilt.

There was an important change in routine before we left. Dr. Donald MacLeod, honorary doctor to the SRU, told us many ways of avoiding injury, preventing skin rashes, staying away from sore stomachs. His advice was invaluable because we did not have a doctor with us and it's the only tour I've been on where none of the players was a doctor, or at least a medical student. A doctor is essential on all tours.

We went first to Thailand and trained the day after arriving. The temperature must have been in the nineties but there were we sweating it out. The locals went into the shade and watched these 'mad dogs and Scotsmen go out in the noonday sun.' The reward was a visit to the night spots of Bangkok. We got back to our hotel feeling that we should be here a few weeks instead of a few days.

The game was as easy as we had imagined it would be. We won 82–3 with all of us trying to pace ourselves to avoid too much exertion in the blistering heat and humidity. Difficult to believe, but some of the boys lost a stone in weight in that 80 minutes. When we came off the field it was as much as we could do just to crawl onto a bench, still wearing our sodden gear. We sat there for about 15 minutes trying to recover. Most of what we lost we replenished that night.

Hong Kong is one of my favourite places in the world. It has a buzz and excitement about it which is unique. It's really a small place but you could never tire of it. There is always something new to see or do or experience every time you go into it.

We trained at a British Army barracks in Hong Kong and were entertained later by a little Welshman. He was rather a comic figure in khaki shorts which were a little too long, and shirt which was a trifle too big. Back in the dressing room after training the banter was good as it always is when a team has worked off its excess energy into a sweat. If the language was a little coarse, was it any different from any other dressing room in any part of the world? We went to a reception that night and met our little Welshman once again. This time he was in uniform—he looked quite different as a reverend. Our chat also took a turn for the proper.

The game against Hong Kong started at 7 pm when the humidity was at its worst. It felt like working in a pressure cooker with the lid on. It was claustrophobic, but if that was bad the referee was worse. We were sweating so much that handling was, to say the least, uncertain. We struggled a bit but in the end we drew away, thanks mainly to Jim Renwick whose class began to tell, and won in the end 49–6. We didn't appreciate a referee who was too fussy, didn't know about advantage, and who made no allowances to let the game flow.

We were happy but so were a delegation from the Japanese Rugby Union who were sponsoring the tour. They had watched us in Bangkok and what they had seen in two games made them confident that we were there for the beating. They were confident after the dinner, and so were we, so it was a happy band— Scottish and Japanese—who left next day for Japan.

Our first game in the land of the rising sun was against the combined universities of Waseda and Meija under floodlight at the Olympic Stadium in Tokyo. The odd thing about some games is that it's sometimes difficult to control them even though you are well ahead as far as possession and planning are concerned. We had planned to play it tight against the universities, draw them in, slow it, then release it when their defence was committed. But it didn't work out that way—how could it against opponents whose tactics were sheer harum-scarum? Their indiscipline seemed to get to us for a while and we played it their way with reckless abandon, but eventually we pulled ourselves together and got back to our plan. We ran out winners by 56–9, but what a lovely night and what a lovely crowd. The result dumbfounded the Japanese delegation who had been following us. Their faces showed that it was not a score which they had expected. Roughly translated, their mutterings were to the effect that we were a Jekyll and Hyde team.

At the after-match function, Tom Pearson wanted to give the universities ties and a plaque but nobody would accept them because they had no presents for us. They were embarrassed. Tom said with a great deal of frankness: 'It's not often that the Scottish Rugby Union can be accused of generosity.'

We travelled to Osaka to play Japan B and stayed at a monastery. Can you imagine it? It's still a bit hard to believe but it was bliss for two days, shattered only by the strident call of Nairn MacEwan for training. There were many of us who were glad to hear that final whistle and to hear the final score of 50–16. Our ever present delegation from the Japan RU were smiling again. Maybe a win against us was possible after all?

To Tokyo and a night life which we would all have loved to join but which we just couldn't afford, apart from a hamburger bar two streets away from the hotel. No wonder we were well prepared and rested for the Test and won by 74–9. We were far too superior and denied them the ball which they craved. The Japanese were inventive, especially in the line-out, and scrummaged well, but eventually gave way to our weight, strength, and technique. They were brave and worthy and their abject dismay at the size of their defeat is something I'll always remember.

Scottish touring team to the Far East, 1977. Ian McLauchlan front row, second from left.

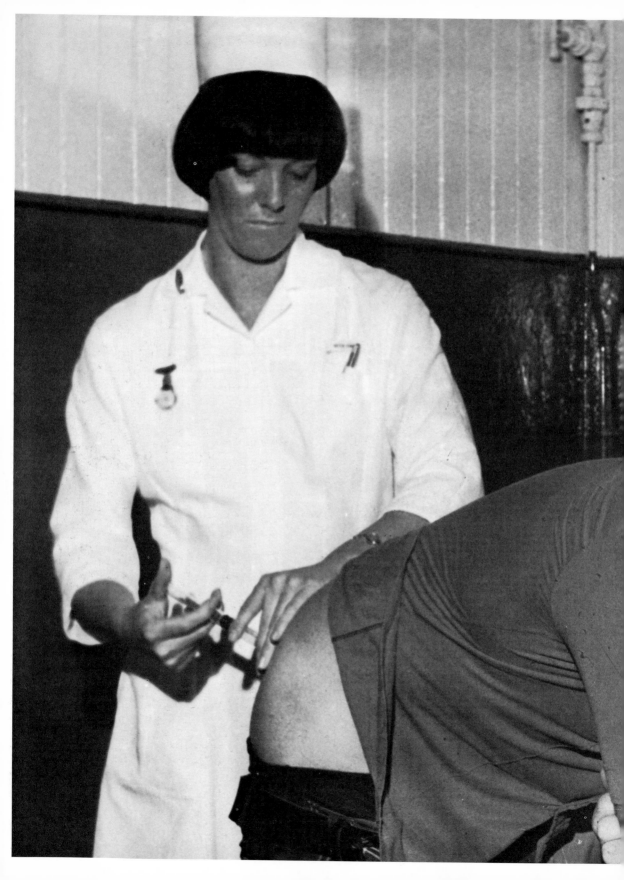

Preparing for the Far East as Jim Renwick looks on.

Our camp followers, the Japan RU, were stunned by the margin but very complimentary in their praise of the Scotland XV. At the dinner it was our turn to be embarrassed. They were extremely generous. I'm sorry they haven't returned to the UK. They learned a lot from us, but they also had a lot to teach as far as handling and speed were concerned.

There was a bitter end to the tour. No arrangement had been made for us to travel home from Heathrow. Some of the boys got on a flight to Edinburgh. Others had to hire a car and drive home.

THE FAMINE

LITTLE DID I realise that when I made my comeback to the Scotland team that I would never again play in a winning team and that it would take Nairn MacEwan 12 full internationals as coach before he experienced the satisfaction of a win. Once, and once only, in his career as coach did Scotland win. We came close several times, but for Nairn the team never delivered the goods which he deserved.

He had been appointed coach on the team's return from the Far East where he had been player coach. He took over from Bill Dickinson who would have been happy to carry on, but some members of the selection committee felt that enough was enough. When it became obvious that the SRU was looking for a replacement for Dickinson it was assumed that Jim Telfer, the coach to the B team, would be appointed. But the SRU passed over the obvious choice.

Dougie Morgan was installed as captain in the 1978 season with myself as pack leader. We could never put things together properly. Our scrummaging was weak and we gave away easy scores in every

Scotland v All Blacks, 1978. Battle for the ball between David Leslie (Scotland) and Gary Sear (N.Z.)

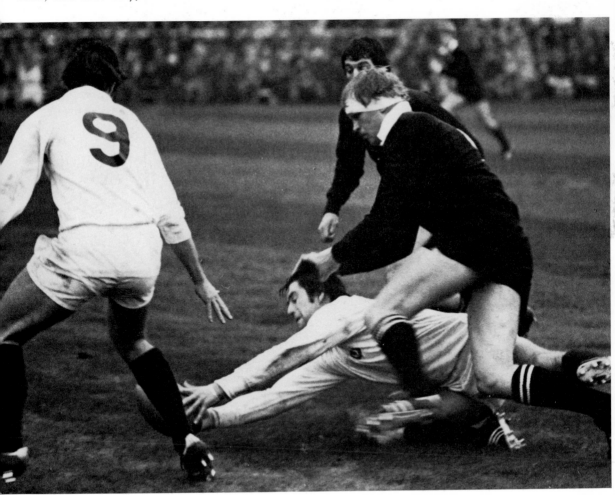

John Rutherford attracts the autograph hunters.

game. Stewart McKinney of Ireland scored from a set scrum; Ray Gravell of Wales ran in untouched after Pender and Tomes collided trying to tackle him; France scored when a kick was dropped; England beat us 15–0 at Murrayfield when most people had the feeling that if they had gone for a teabreak we still wouldn't have scored. We were inept, guileless, clueless.

It was a sad season made even sadder by Sandy Carmichael announcing his retirement having won 50 caps.

Graham Mourie led his All Blacks on to a murky and wet Murrayfield on December 9, 1978, but it looked considerably brighter when Bruce Hay, playing on the left wing, hacked the ball ahead and won the race to the touch down. Andy Irvine converted and we were 6–0 ahead. Could we do it? The murk closed in again when David Leslie, our best forward, was injured and had to be replaced by Ian Lambie, who was winning his first cap. New Zealand then took charge and scored a converted try and two penalties before Ian McGeechan dropped a goal to haul us back into the game at 9–12.

In the dying minutes we won a scrum under the All Blacks posts and Ian McGeechan tried to drop a goal. To our horror, Doug Bruce charged it down and Bruce Robertson picked up the rebound to run the length of the field and score under the posts. It was a desperate piece of misfortune which few spectators saw because it was almost dark.

Wales came to Murrayfield and won by 19–13 without a great deal of exertion and we then achieved some kind of record by drawing twice in one season in

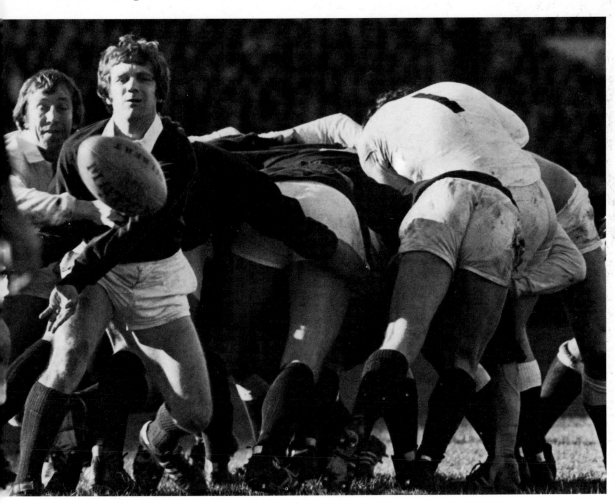

'Too late,' says Dougie Morgan. Scotland v England, 1978.

Dougie Morgan gets the ball safely away v England.

Let me at them. Scotland v New Zealand, 1979.

the Home International championship. At Twickenham, England dominated up front but were poor behind the scrum; we were exactly the opposite. Again a refereeing decision caused some controversy. England were 7–0 ahead when Andy Irvine came into the line and kicked ahead over the England line. As he raced for the touch down he was tripped, but John Rutherford got there and the try was given wide on the left. We thought that Mr. Norling of Wales should have given us a penalty try. Irvine missed the conversion which cost us the result. This was Al McHarg's last game for Scotland so I was the last of the 'old lags.'

Draws in the Home Internationals are difficult to achieve but we made it look easy that season. In Edinburgh, the Irish scrum-half, Colin Paterson, scored two tries from blind-side breaks at set scrums. One is bad; twice is unforgivable. That tied the score at 11–11 and we held our breath while Tony Ward tried to convert Paterson's second try late in the game. Tony did the decent thing and missed.

France beat us by 21–17 in a strange game. We could have won but at the same time we realised that the score against us could have been much worse. We were happy in a way to have escaped a bigger hammering.

The 1979–80 season started with a shock. I was appointed captain to face the All Blacks again on

Andy Irvine breaks against France, 1980.

Confident Scots at Edinburgh Airport.

November 10. I had expected to be in the team but thoughts of captaincy had long gone. Mike Biggar had led us in the Far East and it was assumed that he would lead. I still regard it as one of the greatest honours that can be handed to any sportsman and Nairn MacEwan and I did all we could to bring the boys to a peak for the game. We were pleased with our preparation.

All was going well in the game until Andy Irvine tried to run from defence and was caught by Wilson. The inevitable Mourie was up and drove to our line. The All Blacks won the ruck and Dave Loveridge broke from scrum-half and dummied four Scots to score. It was a soft try and came at the worst possible time—just before half-time. If that was soft, it was nothing to one try in the second-half. Murray Mexted, the No 8, caught the ball in a two-man line-out and ran 25 yards to score without a finger being laid on him. New Zealand scored two further tries and won 20–6, our points coming from two penalties by Andy Irvine.

We had played our hearts out in the forwards but the backs had let us down, especially in defence. After the Press conference, Ian Archer, the well-known sports writer, said that he had never seen me look so disgusted. The sequel was, I suppose, predictable from the SRU—the forwards were blamed and Ian Lambie, Gordon Dickson and myself were dropped against Ireland, Mike Biggar being made captain. The backs remained virtually unchanged the whole season and Scotland never won a game. Andy Irvine had a try at the captaincy, so that in one season Scotland tried three captains. Is this a record?

I was restored to the bench for the game in Wales and again against England at Murrayfield but by that time I was one month off my 38th birthday. I would have loved to go out in an international jersey but I had done my bit. It was time to hand over to younger men in the hope that they would wear the blue shirt and play with the same pride in their country as I had done and would enjoy it as much as I had.

For Nairn MacEwan it was also the end. Unknown to the team he had a heart complaint which required open-heart surgery. He had battled on all season travelling many hundreds of miles to fulfil his duties with the team. He had done a great job which was not perhaps fully appreciated at the time, but his determination to finish the season epitomized his commitment to the Scottish cause. I wish the results had been better for him.

One other thing which struck me in those lean years was the way the crowds flocked to Murrayfield to support the team. At the beginning of the decade there were gaps in the terracing at Murrayfield, especially against France and Ireland. But rugby had become so spectacular that by the end of the 1970s tickets for a Home International were as scarce as Scots at Lords for a Test match against Upper Volta.

I have already described my last game of rugby—at the police ground in Salisbury, Zimbabwe, on June 10th, 1980. After that I turned my attention to coaching which I had previously done as a player. I was very flattered when I was asked to help the Stewarts/Melville club, and I remained with them until my final exclusion from the game.

Over the past two years I have had the opportunity to watch Club rugby in Scotland, and I am afraid that what I see is not too impressive. The overall standard is poor, and I fear that the enlarging of the leagues to fourteen teams will only further the mediocrity; much needs doing to help coaches if the players are to improve their standard of skill and fitness. The inclusion of the Anglo-Scots in the District Championship has helped that competition, but I for one see little point in the home based players travelling to London to play in a District match.

On the International front there are, however, many signs of hope for the future. The same pride and fitness which were the mark of Jim Telfer the player are ever evident in the team that he coaches. The emergence of young forwards such as John Beattie (Glasgow Academicals), Jim Calder (Stewarts/Melville), Derek White (Gala) and Iain Paxton (Selkirk), and the continued improvement of Colin Deans (Hawick) and Iain Milne (Heriots), has given Scotland real pace and ball-winning capacity. Coupled with scrum half Roy Laidlaw (Jedforest), John Rutherford (Selkirk), David Johnston (Watsonians) and Roger Baird (Kelso) they give Scotland a good mixture of speed and awareness which has been lacking over the past few seasons, as well as promising great things for the years to come.

As far as recent Internationals have been concerned, Scotland have played some exceptionally exciting, often suicidal, rugby, and on many occasions it has worked to their advantage: never more so than when they brought off that remarkable win in Cardiff in the last game of 1982 and ran out winners by 30 points to 18. That result, plus the appointment of Jim Telfer as coach to the 1983 British Lions to New Zealand—the first Scot to hold the post—has lifted the stock of Scottish rugby at least at national level.

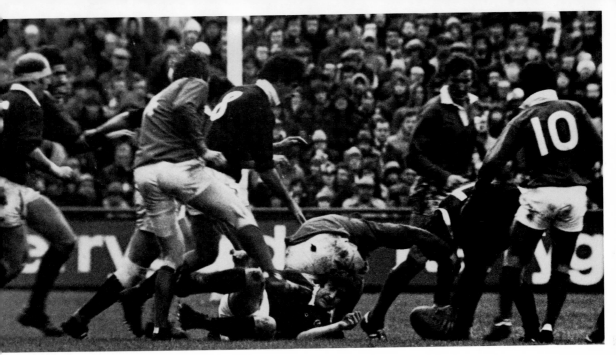

Easy does it, Mossy! Action v Ireland, 1978.

Tackling Fergus Slattery.

INTERNATIONAL PREPARATION

T HE GAME of Rugby Union is an amateur one prepared for and played in a most professional way. The modern game demands dedication and training by the individual over a long period and requires the understanding and help of the player's family. So much time has to be set aside for rugby.

The build-up to the international season actually starts in the close season when most forwards will do distance runs to build stamina and practise with heavy weights to build strength. The backs will also do stamina work and sprint training. When the club season starts there's the usual club training plus extra running and weights for the hopefuls who want to make the international squad. I used to do a minimum of half an hour each night. Added to that there were the international squad weekends involving the leading 40 players in the country.

We would meet on a Friday evening for those weekends and we listened to talks by the chairman of selectors and the coach. The weekend then usually went like this:

SATURDAY
9.30 am   Assemble. Warm-up. Unopposed practice concentrating on individual and unit skills.
12.30 pm   Lunch.
2 pm   Reassemble. Warm-up. Opposed individual and unit skills.
4 pm   Conditioned game with three teams—two playing, one watching. The teams are rotated.
5.30 pm   End of practical session. Shower.
7.30 pm   Evening meal and post-mortem on day's work.

SUNDAY
9.30 am   Assemble and warm-up.
10.00 am   Fitness tests, basic skills and practice and games.

12.30 pm   Fitness advice and individual training schedules handed out.
1 pm   Lunch and dispersal.

These sessions would take place late in August and perhaps two or three Sunday sessions would be held in October and November when the fitness of the players would be monitored. There would occasionally be changes in personnel attending the sessions.

In addition to playing and training with his club, the internationalist is involved in a District team which also holds squad sessions, perhaps on a Wednesday or a Sunday when clubs are not training.

When the players are finally selected for the National team, having gone through club and district matches, they meet at Murrayfield on the Sunday morning before an international.

9.30 am   Assemble. Outline of the day by coach.
10 am   Change and warm-up.
FORWARDS—scrummaging against machine and live opposition—at least 50 scrums. Concentrate on blocking and driving at the line-out. Ruck and maul from scrum and line-out.
BACKS—handling quickly to wings, passing, supporting, concentrating on the speed of the ball through the hands. Handling at full speed.
1 pm   Team comes together for semi-opposed game controlled by the coach. Talk by coach about the game the following Saturday.
2 pm   Lunch and dispersal. During the week the player, depending on the individual, trains on Tuesday.

THURSDAY
11 am   Assemble.
11.30 am   Change, warm-up, talk by coach. Forwards scrummage, line-out, ruck, maul.
12.30 pm   Backs practise handling, defence, counter-attack.
1.15 pm   Unopposed concentration on attack.
1.30 pm   Short penalties, etc., then lunch.
In the afternoon the team watches video recordings of the opposition and the evenings are free.

FRIDAY
10.30 am   Team meeting at hotel to go through codes, penalties, and defence.
11.15 am   Bus to Murrayfield. Change and warm-up. Short session on defence and attacking ploys.

Front row union: Carmichael, Madsen and me.

Colin Telfer, exhausted by the training, has to be carried.

Relaxation during training with David Johnston.

Big lift for new cap, David Johnston.

French journalists watch scrummage session with Bill
Dickinson.

Scrum – scrum – scrum.

12.45 pm	Bus back to hotel for lunch. The rest of the day is free.

SATURDAY

11 am	Team meeting at the hotel for final preparation.
11.45 am	Lunch.
12.45 pm	Bus to Murrayfield where we usually arrive at about 1 pm. Change and warm-up in dressing room.
2 pm	Kick-off.

During the hour before the game, the players prepare themselves physically and mentally.

The coach and the captain go round the players building the atmosphere so that when the team runs out to the roar of 70,000 people they are ready for anything. Once on the pitch, the nerves disappear—from the kick-off the action is so fast and furious that nerves are forgotten. After the game there's the usual exchange of shirts with the opposition—I've got a collection of about 60 international and club shirts—and thanks for the game.

In my time we had a ritual back at the hotel where the dinner was to be held. A room was set aside for the players, officials, and coach, and there we talked among ourselves for about an hour. This was sheer therapy—we talked the game out of our systems. We said what we wanted to say. Nothing went beyond that room. When we left that room we had nothing more to say about the match. We weren't letting off steam to anybody else. We weren't going to say anything indiscreet to the Press. We then went to the dinner, and had a great time, and on the Sunday we dispersed.

Bill lays it on the line.

Weight training for the season.

SUPER SCOTS

SCOTLAND HAVE won the Grand Slam only once in their history. The Triple Crown has come their way eight times, the last time being 1938. It's a dismal record when you consider the marvellous Scots who have played and won and lost but never seen a sight of a Triple Crown. Men like Ken Scotland, Arthur Smith, David Rollo, Hughie MacLeod, Gordon Waddell, Ronnie Glasgow. In my time we came close, in 1973 and 1975.

There have always been vital weaknesses in all of our teams but I'm going to suggest the best 14 Scottish players I have played with. Had they been together in the same XV they would have swept the boards.

As always, the choice is wide and difficult for many of the positions. Bruce Hay or Andy Irvine at fullback? Bruce was one of the bravest players I've ever met. He feared nothing and his tackling in defence was immense. Many looked on him as a defensive player, pure and simple, but when he burst into the line he was practically unstoppable. Scotland played both Hay and Irvine in the same team—as the Lions did—as winger and fullback, and I for one believe that we could have developed an extremely effective twin fullback game which would have used Bruce's defensive qualities and Andy's attacking flair more fully. My choice for fullback would, however be Andy.

He is not and never claimed to be a defensive player. In fact, some of his tackling at international level left a lot to be desired. But what he did have was the ability to create space and cause the opposition to

Bill Cuthbertson eyes down on the ball v France.

panic when he started to run from the deep. His timing of coming into the line was immaculate. He seemed to 'ghost' in, as if coming from nowhere. The 'try' he scored against Wales in 1981 at Murrayfield was a case in point.

Bruce Hay on the left wing fly-hacked a loose Welsh pass and from nowhere Andy appeared to race Gareth Davies to the line for the ball. Davies obstructed Andy and a penalty try was given, but I'm convinced that no other player in the world would have anticipated that situation and reacted as quickly as Irvine, and that is what makes him one of the all-time greats of world rugby.

The two wingers I'd pick are Dave Shedden of West of Scotland and Keith Robertson of Melrose. Neither was an out-and-out flier in terms of pace but each was a great footballer. Who could forget Shedden's covering tackle on David Duckham at Murrayfield in 1976 when he crossed the field to save a certain try? In the same game he caught a kick ahead and started the counter-attack from deep inside the 22 which led to Alan Lawson scoring the first of his tries in that memorable win.

Keith Robertson is one of the most complete footballers who ever played for Scotland. He could play on both wings, centre, fullback, and out-half, and his awareness of players around him made him exceptional. Other wingers could be considered, like Billy Steele, that elegant 'dancer' as we called him in South Africa, and the big men like Alastair Biggar and Mike Smith who I felt never had the attacking and defensive awareness of Robertson and Shedden.

For centre, many good players come to mind. Chris Rae, Jock Turner, Ian McGeechan and Jim Renwick all performed well on Lions tours while John Frame, Alastair Cranston, David Johnston, David Bell and Ian Forsyth were all great to play with. One wonders just how far the uncapped Ian Murchie would have gone had injury not curtailed his career.

But the combination of Jim Renwick, the most capped centre in the world, and Jock Turner of Gala would be my choice. Renwick, who like good wine improves with age, has the ability to beat men by running, kicking, or passing. His acceleration off the mark is exceptional. Turner, like Robertson, could play anywhere in the back line. His reading of the

Big Al plunges over for a try v France.

Bill Cuthbertson, Norrie Rowan and Colin Deans
watch the ball safely back as Willie Duggan (Ireland)
looks on.

France v Scotland, 1981.

game and strength in the middle of the field meant that he could shrug off tackles or hold the ball long enough to bring his forwards to him. His rugged tackling was the feature of his game and had he made himself available would most certainly have gone to New Zealand with the 1971 Lions. His decision to retire from rugby at an early age was a great blow to Scotland.

Combination is a prime consideration when picking half-backs. The pair must complement each other. Such a pair—Roy Laidlaw of Jedforest and John Rutherford of Selkirk are my choice. Each is so different yet they play so well together. Laidlaw is the small, gritty, aggressive scrum-half who loves to break close and take on the opposing forwards. He snaps at the heels of his pack and deals so competently with any kind of possession. Rutherford is the tall and elegant out-half who ghosts through gaps and kicks with a beautifully balanced action which has the stamp of class.

Others who have played with distinction are Gordon Connell and Colin Telfer who did so well in Australia. Dunc Paterson and Ian Robertson perhaps didn't get the quality possession that they needed but then I also have to pass over Douglas Morgan, the

most competitive and cunning scrum-half, and Alan Lawson of the enormous swinging pass and the quick decisive break.

The tight-head prop, allowing that I would pick myself for the loose-head, would be Sandy Carmichael. There's just no argument for that position. He was, technically, the best scrummager and his tackling and speed around the field were second to none. His work rate often wasn't fully appreciated by those who didn't play with him; he just did the job with the minimum of fuss and he did it superbly well.

Hooker presents more of a problem. On pure hooking chores, Duncan Madsen was probably the best ball winner and in the art of putting pressure on the opposition he would again come out on top. Overall, however, one couldn't go past Colin Deans, the Hawick flier who has improved all aspects of his play in the tight while his speed around the field is of enormous value to any side.

The boiler house of the scrum, the second row,

Jim Renwick on the burst, challenged by French captain Jean-Pierre Rives. John Rutherford and Keith Robertson in close support, while Jim Calder waits.

David Leslie ready to pounce v Wales.

Non-stop Roy Laidlaw feeds John Rutherford v Ireland.

The exciting new talent Roger Baird is almost away against France.

picks itself. Gordon Brown and Al McHarg were the perfect blend and they gave the Scotland team stability and ball winning capacity in all aspects during the early 1970s. Brown was the best scrummaging lock I ever played with and was the perfect partner for 'Big Al,' who, though a good scrummager, played a looser game elsewhere. 'Broon Frae Troon' was just a pure donkey, which is a complimentary term for a great tight forward. While he was in rucking the ball out from somebody's foot, McHarg would be there in the centre to receive a pass and make an overlap. How many other second-row men have you seen like McHarg who would do his job in a scrum and seconds later be making a mark underneath his own posts? Big Al was unique and was never fully appreciated.

P. C., Gordon's elder brother, was also a good second-row man. He scrummaged well and was also a line-out master. He changed to No 8 but was, in my opinion, a better lock. Ian Barnes, the Hawick heavy man, was one of the best forwards ever to represent Scotland. Though not the keenest trainer in the world, Barney was always there or thereabouts when the ball went loose. He used to say: 'You'll beat me at running up and down a field but I'll always get to the ball first.' He and his Hawick clubmate, Alan Tomes, were both good players who lacked that little bit of self confidence to be really great.

I must not forget the gentle giant, Peter Stagg, who never seemed to take the game very seriously, David Gray, the young West of Scotland lock who may yet make the grade, nor Bill Cuthbertson of Kilmarnock who grafted remorselessly to make his place and keep it. He is a little on the small side for a lock but makes

Derek White tackles and Jim Calder has his eye on the loose ball.

Sandy Carmichael in action.

Stewarts/Melville v Heriots – one of the top games in
the league.

Willie John McBride bursts clear v England.

up for that by hard work and commitment.

The No 8 position brings in people like Jim Telfer, Gordon Strachan, Kenny Oliver, and P. C. Brown. Strachan was a hard man of great physical strength who was never really given a chance to prove his true worth to Scotland. That was a pity because he had all the attributes of a great player.

Jim Telfer it would have to be for my team of Super Scots because he was a hard man who never spared himself on the field and was enormously proud of playing for Scotland. Telfer never gave up—there are many who thought he had a death wish—such was his fervour for the game. He was a good ball winner in the line-out and a great rucking forward. He would dive in head first to capture the ball from opponents' feet and think nothing of it.

For flankers, just look at the choice. It's like an embarrassment of riches. Nairn MacEwan, Gordon Dickson, David Leslie—all from Gala—Tom Elliot (Langholm), Roger Arneil (Leicester), Wilson Lauder (Neath), Mike Biggar (London Scottish). Difficult to pick just two from that lot but I would finally have to go for Leslie and MacEwan. Leslie for his explosive speed, aggressive tackling and ball winning capability in the line-out and on the ground. MacEwan, quite simply, was the best left side flanker in the game.

So, my team of Super Scots would be: Irvine, Robertson, Turner, Renwick, Shedden; Rutherford, Laidlaw; McLauchlan, Deans, Carmichael, G. Brown, McHarg, MacEwan, Telfer, Leslie.

Irvine with Hay in close support.

Scotland v Wales. Hold it!

The 'Mouse' finds the hole.

Scotland v Wales. All eyes on Big Al as he scoops up the ball.

Scotland v England. Barry Nelmes grabs Mike Biggar's head.

Stack Stevens of England fells Dougie Morgan at Twickenham.

Alan Lawson about to swing out a pass.

Tony Neary of England tackles Dougie Morgan.

Awarding a trophy . . .   . . . and receiving one from Tom Hovie, Glasgow
                                           Chairman.

Signing in before the International—myself, Duncan
Madsen, Nairn MacEwan and Hamish Bryce.

Jay Crawford and Bill Torrance of Radio Forth help
me give away £1,000.

All set for the Edinburgh Marathon, 1982.